GET PAST YOUR SH*T

Nineteen Stories Of Imperfect People Who Prove You Can

A COLLABORATION ORGANIZED
BY KELLY MCCAUSEY

Paperback: ISBN 978-1-947366-00-8
Ebook: ISBN 978-1-947366-01-5

Library of Congress Control Number: 2020915815

First Paperback Edition: October 2020

Collaboration Organizer: Kelly McCausey
Editorial Advisor: Candice L. Davis
Story Coach: Karin Crompton
Cover Art: Samantha Angel

Published by
Shminkle, LLC
P. O Box 47
Bath, MI 48808

GetPastYourShit.com

TABLE OF CONTENTS

Acknowledgments

When I decided to invite others into a book collaboration with me, I knew I could never do it alone. I want to thank some truly amazeballs people.

Karin Crompton, who worked alongside us all as a Story Coach. Her coaching, writing suggestions, and ever curious questions have helped us all share the most powerful stories we can.

Candice L. Davis, who served as an Editorial Advisor. She brought her publishing expertise to bear on our decisions every step of the way. I can't tell you the peace and confidence I gained from having her available.

I also want to thank Michelle Aubin, Sandy Lawrence, Samantha Angel, Pam Hamilton, Lynn Leusch, and Tishia Lee for providing incredible support for the entire project. You stepped up to love the project as much as I do and I appreciate you for it.

Foreword

For most of my life, I hid.

I was an expert, at least in my mind, of illusions. On the outside, I attempted to look like I had it all together and yet, on the inside, it was rapidly falling apart – my marriage, my finances, my health, my dreams. My ego wouldn't let anyone know that I was scrambling. Instead, it worked tirelessly to patch gaping holes that might expose the unraveling on the inside.

Honestly, I lived in fear. Fear of knocks on the door that would bring bill collectors. Fear of the mail and late notices. Fear of people coming over and seeing how run down everything was inside. Fear of talking with others and them knowing we had no money. Fear of sharing about the parts of that marriage that were not healthy.

Fear is a powerful tool that lies to us. It says, "Play it safe, don't try, what if you get hurt?" In some ways, fear seems safer, like a giant roll of bubble wrap protecting our hearts from another painful encounter.

But fear also keeps us stuck.

It keeps us hiding.

It keeps us in denial.

It keeps us pretending.

It keeps us making excuses.

It keeps us living a life on hold.

It keeps us waiting.

It keeps us jealous.

It keeps us existing.

Fear tells us to believe that life is what it is.

Fear makes us believe we are powerless.

Fear is a liar.

There was a moment ten years ago when I knew I couldn't keep up the façade any longer. I was exhausted from it all, was losing hope, but knew I needed to keep showing up for my kids. I didn't want this story to become their story. I didn't have any answers, didn't know the solution, but knew that I couldn't keep waiting for good to happen – I had to be the catalyst of change.

This change wasn't external, but rather, a deep internal mindset shift. It was me driving a stake in the ground and saying to myself, "There is no going back. You are strong; you matter."

Fear subtly teaches us all to forget our worth. It erases the amazing things we've done and replaces them with worries about what could happen and how potentially bad it could be. It convinces us that it's safer and wiser to wait or to play it safe. It makes us fear others' reactions more than our own hearts.

The antidote to fear is bravery.

Not the loud kind of brave that we see in movies, but rather the small moment when instead of ignoring an issue, we look at it; when instead of thinking we've failed, we see our strength; when instead of waiting, we try.

Bravery replaces the doubts with the truth of knowing that we are enough.

The unwavering decision to change my life began with one thing: worth. I realized that life was going to keep moving no matter what, and that I could live my entire life watching it pass by. I didn't want to be one who waited. Those people seemed bitter, angry at life for dealing them a bad hand.

The thing is – there are people who win at poker with the worst hand because they believe they can bluff everyone else into believing their hand is the best. Somehow their worst hand becomes a winning hand. Did they change the cards? Or did they decide to use their skills?

Truthfully, in those days I was stuck. But I knew somebody could figure a way out and I didn't want to let fear limit me and make me one who believed I couldn't. So I started to play the game of life differently. Taking risks, taking steps, being vulnerable.

Vulnerability is often the catalyst for tremendous change.

Instead of hiding my life, I began to write about it on my blog, Finding Joy. I wrote about motherhood and my emotions and struggling to find worth. In some ways, I was, as Kelly said, "getting over my own shit." In the process of writing I began to develop courage to do the hard things. Courage to say no to unhealthy relationships, to confront and fix my finances, to change my personal story. I also forged priceless connections, began doing the things I thought I couldn't do, and began taking risks.

It wasn't that I just changed my mind – I changed my actions.

I believed in my worth.

I believed life is a gift.

I believed I would never regret trying.

I believed I was enough.

Now, ten years later, I'm happier than I ever have been. I am remarried to an amazing man who loves not only me but also my children. We created a company that provides for us and gives us the freedom to stay home with the kids. My website, Finding Joy, has received more than fifty million pageviews and our Facebook page reaches millions each week. We own a beautiful home and I no longer live with fear as a posture of life.

Several years ago I secured a book deal with Penguin Random House and wrote a self-help book/memoir called, "The Brave Art of Motherhood." This book is a guide on how to get over your own excuses and change your story. I vulnerably shared how I was stuck and how changing my mindset and putting plans into action changed my life. As irony would have it, I wound up on the *Today Show* sharing about my book, but more specifically how I moved from poverty to financial success.

What I once hid had become my voice of hope.

No longer was there shame over money, but rather my words and story were of empowerment and encouragement.

That is what this book is for you.

Think of it as your reminder that we as humans can do hard things. Everyone in this book shares a common thread – vulnerability. Their openness and willingness to expose the struggle and then how they overcame fear to change their lives is a reminder that no matter where you start, you have the opportunity to change tomorrow.

Don't let fear whisper to you, telling you to wait until tomorrow to do the hard things. Life will pass you by. You are given a choice. That's what Kelly wants you to see: that choice, to either wait or to live with fervor and purpose.

It starts with you.

You can read the stories and think, "That's nice, that worked for them, but not me." Or you can read them and be inspired to silence your ego and its fear-talking voice and to let the true you, the brave spirit within, shine.

Life is too short to wait.

I believe in you. Kelly believes in you.

It's your time.

Rachel Marie Martin

INTRODUCTION

Ego And Essence

Have you ever heard someone exclaim, "I'm so tired of all this shit!"

Have you shouted it yourself?

Maybe you were talking about circumstances or other people, but I discovered something key a few years ago: if I'm constantly frustrated, overwhelmed, and downright angry about something – it's not about circumstances and other people.

It's about me.

I'm so tired of all of MY shit.

My shit is my Ego in overdrive.

During our lives, we move between Ego and Essence. Ego is made up of the rules we pick up, the programming we take on, the fears, insecurities, and hang-ups that influence and limit us.

Essence is the part of us that explores, creates, and loves with joyful openness. It's our natural state of being. We're born with it.

Ego wants only to protect us from hurt and harm. Essence wants only to experience all there is and express our unique gifts.

They work gloriously together... until they don't.

For me, a childhood fraught with distrust and abuse resulted in my Ego grabbing control. But it surpassed its wonderful purpose of keeping me alive to instead wrap me in fear about the world and all the people in it – worse, it made up false truths about me.

Ego choked out Essence whenever it might put me at risk of failure and rejection.

My shit is all the ways my Ego operates outside of its true purpose:

- Fear where my life isn't actually at risk
- Insecurity that makes me look for security anywhere outside of myself and my God
- Made-up rules that cause me to judge others and turn it all back on myself
- Doubt about my potential
- Anxiety about my future
- Worry about my past
- Shame about my mistakes

We all have shit.

People who study these things estimate our thoughts are 98 percent based in Ego. That is a whole lot of fear, insecurity, worry, shame, and focus on trying to get something right – and it describes my life from childhood into my forties.

Can you relate?

Ego plays a crazy-making game with us.

First, it identifies all the reasons we're getting things wrong. Then it makes lists of all the things we could do to get it right. Then it makes new accusations every step of the way, always keeping the idea of being enough as we are just out of reach.

It sounds awful and abusive, and isn't that exactly what it is? Self-abuse? Self-sabotage?

It's like my Ego says, "Hey, yeah, make that list, do the things, it will work this time!" just to set me up for another take-down, returning to find fault and point out mistakes, saying, "Sorry sister, good try, you still suck!"

My life until forty-seven was spent in this terrible cycle of pulling myself up by my bootstraps, working a plan, and seeing it come crashing down. Maybe I'd get a step in the right direction every few years, but I always felt disappointed – mostly in myself.

Ego doesn't want a win. For the Ego, winning means staying right where you are.

As uncomfortable as here is, it's predictable and Ego knows how to protect you when it knows the playing field. Of all that Ego can do, it cannot be creative.

I learned about Ego and Essence when I went to a Radical Leadership retreat at forty-seven. My first goal was to learn how to make more confident decisions. I knew I spent way too much time weighing options, gathering opinions – I wanted to know better for myself what I wanted to do. Hell, I wanted to know what I wanted.

A secondary goal, one that fluttered on my lips unexpectedly when asked... I wanted to know how to love myself. I felt like a stranger to love. As much as I felt love for others, and as often as I felt loved by others, I didn't have any experience of loving myself. How could I? With so many failures, with such up-close awareness of my own brokenness and ugliness of thought? I felt unlovable.

As the retreat helped us focus on seeing ways Ego and Essence show up in our lives, I found the answer to my self-love question.

It was crystal clear: Ego ran my life and Ego isn't capable of love.

Only Essence can love, and Essence isn't found in following rules or getting it right. Essence just loves.

There's no work to be done. There's only willingness to accept it.

It's not earned or deserved or lost or gained. It is who we are.

We are love.

I am love.

At least, when I'm not letting my shit get in the way.

When I get past my shit, I get to experience love and every other good thing I want to create in life – and so can you.

In this book, you'll read nineteen stories of people who have gotten past their shit. The specifics of their stories are different, but you'll start noticing the thread: of an Ego that had spun out of control until each person found a way to reconnect to Essence.

My hope is that you'll see yourself in this book and will be inspired to find your Essence, too.

Love, Kelly McCausey

CHAPTER ONE

Not Hiding Behind My Shit Anymore

Kelly McCausey

I used to believe we could find the one big reason any of us struggles with life and be fixed – good to go forever more. Now I know that idea is a fool's errand. There is never just one WHY.

When I think about it, I've got at least some shit about everything.

My Shit About Being Unloved

I was adopted and I've always known it.

So it was confusing when I was thirteen and met a woman at a family gathering who exclaimed, "She looks just like her!"

Who? I didn't look at all like anyone in my family. Later, a relative filled me in: my birth mother was my uncle's stepdaughter and the person I'd just met was my birth mother's cousin.

I don't know the whole story. With only fragments of family gossip to work with, what I understand about my biological mother is this: Married before 18, already a mother to one and with a husband in Vietnam, she got pregnant with another man's child. Faced with losing what little she had, she chose to let me go.

My learning about the family connection meant I could probably find her if I tried. (Spoiler: While I did indeed locate her and seek contact, first at seventeen and again in my early twenties, I was firmly rebuffed and we've never met.)

The news also brought waves of anger. How could my uncle and his wife, the entire family, and everyone who knew my adoptive mother, support giving her a tiny baby?

Ahhh, but they didn't know her like I did. The rest of the world saw what she wanted them to, but two of us — one of my brothers and me — knew what she was capable of.

She physically and emotionally abused me my entire life. I had no experience of a warm family home, a safe place to be, or a loving mother's arms around me.

My parents raised me to know I was adopted. We had a little set of books about it, one for the parents and one for the child. My dad read me the book many times. It said I was so special that I was chosen. It said I was loved and wanted.

My dad made the book feel true for me, but I wonder what my little mind made of that book and what I was experiencing of mom. I didn't believe at all that she wanted me and certainly never felt loved.

An older sibling tells me I was a momma's girl as a baby. Maybe she was a loving and attentive mother to a little one she had taken in as her own? There is nothing in my experience to support it.

Did you ever see the movie *Mommie Dearest*? It tells the story of Christina Crawford and her adoptive mother, actress Joan Crawford. There's a scene in the movie where Christina is woken and beaten with a wire hanger. Every stitch of clothing in her closet is thrown on the floor for her to take care of.

I had a bizarrely similar experience, minus the wire hanger thankfully. My mother found my underwear drawer looking unorganized – which was against the rules. She dumped every item out of every drawer and the entire closet too. I was to put everything back perfectly as my punishment, and be grounded for the rest of the week.

I was always grounded. Always. Often sent to bed early when neighborhood children were playing with my brother in the yard, I watched so much fun through my bedroom window growing up.

Mom used a leather belt for the smallest infractions, applied to the backs of my legs as often as my buttocks, sometimes leaving terrible welts that would take days to heal. I wore long pants in warm weather to hide them from others.

If it was unusual at thirteen to still be getting "spankings," I did not know it, but the last time my mother physically hurt me involved a shove that sent me tumbling back over furniture. The fall cracked my tailbone, creating an explosion of pain and difficulty sitting down for weeks.

Saying I received an actual injury is only an assumption, as she didn't take me to be seen.

We certainly never talked about it, but somehow that experience changed things. The leather belt remained on top of the fridge but I was never sent to bring it again.

Over the years, I've been asked if I believe my abuse was related to being adopted and my answer is no. If I'd been born of her body, my experience is likely to have been the same. One of my brothers can surely attest to it.

What I didn't know then is that my mother was an alcoholic. I thought she wanted to hurt me, knew I could not please her, and I imagined she hated me. I couldn't know then that she probably hated herself.

Just like my birth mother, my adoptive mother was married before eighteen. Within a few years, she had three children and felt miserably unhappy. Seven years before I was born, she left her little family to run away with my father. A private investigator found her six months later, pregnant with her fourth child.

It was a scandalous situation for sure in the late 1950s. Her husband divorced her and filed abandonment papers. She fought back, demanding visitation with her children and winning it – though it did not last. Her oldest child ultimately came to live with her but the younger kids stopped visiting after a short while.

Do you wonder, like I do, how a woman legally abandons children and is allowed to adopt another? This is a mystery to me to this day.

My father was also an alcoholic, though he was the classic stumbling drunk with an amiable disposition even when full of beer. At least that's my memory of it. Dad coming home drunk, late – mom being mad. Dad always with a paper sack-covered quart between his legs, driving down the road with us kids.

My parents divorced when I was nine – a devastating thing for me, as my father's presence was the only respite from mom's relentless abuse. He quit drinking after that, his only way to gain visitation with us kids. Knowing what I know about alcoholism today, it's a miracle, isn't it? He never drank again, remaining sober until he died when I was nineteen.

My father's alcoholism and sobriety made the discovery that mom was an alcoholic hard to understand. Dad drank beer openly and his demeanor made it obvious. Mom, it turns out, was a closet drinker. And I never knew.

All those glasses of iced tea she nursed were Long Island Iced Teas. She was drinking all day long. After I moved out at sixteen, I learned from a sibling that she kept small bottles of alcohol in the car, in the lockers at work, in the bedroom closet.

I had no clue, all those times mom was verbally abusing me, beating me, sending me to bed early, grounding me and refusing to allow friends to visit, that she was functionally drunk, completely addicted... and keeping us isolated at home served that purpose.

I remember feeling stunned at the time. Over the years, the information offered me a gift of perspective: It wasn't all about me; it was about her. She was clearly hurting and constantly self-medicating. She was barely managing to love herself, is it any wonder she couldn't love me?

Hell, maybe she did love me. She died more than ten years ago and I still don't really know. We never had one real conversation about my childhood, her treatment of me, or her alcoholism.

Here's the thing: it doesn't actually matter whether she did. I didn't feel love from her and I made so much up about myself in that experience:

- I am unwanted.
- I am unloved.
- I am unlovable.
- I am broken.
- I am fundamentally not acceptable.
- I am a pain in the ass.

I blamed mom for making me think all of these things about myself and wished I could have experienced a different life. For so long I thought if I had had a loving mother, I'd be a different person. And because I had the life I did, I couldn't be loved and lovable.

These once-accepted beliefs and the Ego-based thoughts are the fears, insecurities, and self-protective mechanisms that try to hold me back.

Essence plows through all of it with love, taking me past my shit about being unloved.

My Shit About Being Fat

I wasn't a fat kid. Far from it, I was deliciously normal.

I was five feet, seven inches and weighed about 135 pounds at thirteen. I had an athletic build with strong legs from an active childhood. If I met a girl today who looked just like me, I'd never think of her as fat.

By my teen years I picked up the idea that I was fat – and not very pretty.

At home I was aware that my mother was constantly dieting. Her ongoing battle with twenty or so extra pounds ruled our kitchen and poured into my life as she criticized my food choices and how I looked in clothing.

At school I compared myself to girls with slender body types and became convinced I was doing something wrong, eating something wrong, not moving enough, needing to do something different to be accepted.

By sixteen I was 150.

By eighteen I was 160.

I started telling myself I couldn't do certain things.

- I can't flirt with the guy I like because I'm not pretty enough. I'll do it when my hair is longer or I can wear more makeup and feel prettier.
- I can't try out for a dancing role in the school play because I'm not very coordinated. I'm downright clumsy, everyone knows that.
- I can't wear those shorts because my legs are too fat. I'll wear cute clothes when I lose weight.

A guy I liked told me I was a "big girl" and he usually dated "smaller chicks." I internalized the idea that I needed to be skinny to be loved.

The more I focused on the idea that I wasn't doing something right, the more I obsessed about how I should be doing something different, the more I dieted (and fell off of diets), and the heavier I got.

I was 185 at twenty-three.

230 at twenty-eight.

300 at thirty-five.

369 at fifty.

My Shit About Being Seen

The internet opened the door of my dreams. On the internet I could be myself, write my words, speak my thoughts, give my advice, make friends, and feel connected – all without anyone ever knowing I'm FAT.

I started my business in 2002, back when we didn't even put photos online; we used cartoon avatars. When we did start using photos, I would take a hundred pictures until I got one, of my face only, that made me look as slim as possible.

While my business projects grew, I stayed hidden. While some of my friends were traveling to do in-person things, I stayed home behind excuses that I couldn't possibly go. Truthfully, if someone had made every way possible for me, I would have still said no. I did not want anyone to see me and know that I'm FAT.

My business partner traveled across the country for an event just three hours away from me and I wouldn't go meet her. I couldn't bear being seen.

In 2008 I was invited to speak on a panel at a big new media event out in California. It was a great honor, a wonderful opportunity... and I said no. The thought of stepping on a stage was humiliating.

The internet was faster than ever and more people were doing video – which I shied away from as long as possible. I did not want to be seen for who I was.

My insecurities screamed inside.

- Nobody wants to see a fat person on stage.
- Nobody will respect me if they know I'm this fat.
- Nobody wants to be on a plane next to a big fat woman like me.
- People think all fat people are lazy and dumb.

These thoughts crippled me and held firmly in place while it seemed the rest of the world moved forward and enjoyed opportunities.

Something finally broke for me in 2009. This was long before I tackled any mindset work. I had just had enough of my chicken behavior and decided it was time to face my fears.

I went to my first in-person event with about 150 people in attendance. It felt safe in some ways because I knew enough people who I felt would love me no matter what. I felt terrifyingly vulnerable around everyone else.

My internal dialogue throughout the event was exhausting.

- He probably thinks I'm an ugly cow.
- That guy won't want me to sit next to him.
- I can't go sit down, there isn't an extra chair on either side to give me space.

- She doesn't even recognize me. I'm so fat in person she can't tell it's me.
- If I eat this snack, will everyone think I'm always stuffing my face?
- Don't reach for that dessert, you fatty.
- I wonder if she's sorry she asked me to join her for lunch. Is she embarrassed to be seen with me?

This was my shit – but I was getting past it.

Despite wanting desperately to hide in my hotel room every minute, I forced myself to remain among others, and not just those I knew. I demanded of myself to be social with strangers, to risk the worst rejections, and to make the most of the event.

It was a turning point in my life, not just for my business. It was empowering to step past every awful thought to DO something I wanted to do.

Did some people judge me? I have no doubt. Did I hear any ugly whispers? Only in the airport from strangers. Might someone I know have said something like "I didn't know she was so fat!" behind closed doors? In my imagination, for sure. In reality, I have no idea.

Did I imagine the worst? Yes, constantly.

Did the worst happen? No. I had a wonderful time in spite of the rolling tape of shit in my head.

I returned to that event the following year as an instructor and I continued to speak there for several years afterward and began pursuing other speaking opportunities.

With every new event I attended and every stage I stepped on, my shit has continued to run.

My thoughts love to predict what other people are thinking.

- Wow, she's REALLY fat.
- Fat people make me uncomfortable. (I've heard that one said.)
- I don't want to sit by her. Please don't let her come sit by me.
- I can't put her on stage, she's enormous!
- Anybody that fat is probably a slob. I don't want to work with someone with so little self-control.

For as many whispers as I have picked up on and imagined over the years, something overshadows them.

Every time I have spoken in person, a large woman has come to thank me for showing her it is possible. They say things like:

- I've never seen a fat woman on a stage before. I'm so inspired!
- Now that I've seen you do it, I'm willing to try.
- Seeing someone who looks like me doing something so brave, my excuses are falling away.

These conversations, emails, and private messages are a gift to me and have helped me take the next big step past my own shit.

All of the years I was going to other events, people would ask me when I was hosting my own. I'd always say "No way!" I felt completely intimidated by the idea... but I knew why they asked.

Online, I'm a community leader. I create spaces for people to meet, learn, co-operate, and grow. It is only natural I'd want to do the same with in-person events – but my shit was standing in the way.

- Nobody wants to come to an event hosted by a fat woman.
- Speakers won't want to be associated with my event.
- People will lose respect for me if they spend too much time with me in person. My weight will be in their face all day for three days and they'll want to run away.

Yeah, these thoughts get ridiculous, but that's how shit works. It takes every fear to the nth degree – whatever it takes to keep you from stepping out and experiencing all that fear.

In 2013 I started hosting my own in-person multi-speaker events. Because I got past my shit, I've now hosted or co-hosted twelve in-person multi-speaker events and thirteen in-person retreats.

Because I didn't let my shit run me, I've had powerful up-close-and-personal impacts. I have hugged hundreds of amazing people, welcomed them into a beautiful safe space, invited them to grow into their best self, and equipped them to build successful businesses.

Side note: Do you know I used to claim not to be a hugger? For years I believed it myself. In truth, it was my shit talking.

- Nobody wants to hug your fat body.
- Your fat probably grosses him out.
- Don't act like you want a hug, act like you hate hugs.
- Just shake her hand, don't impose your fat on her.

Shit lies.

Of course, we know our fears and insecurities lie – but we struggle to know when something is or isn't untrue.

As I've taken more uncomfortable steps and fallen in love with what I used to run away from, I've been reexamining some of my most inaccurate beliefs about myself.

I'm pretty sure I used to claim I'm not a people person. That's hilarious!

Shit makes me say things I don't mean. Or at the very least, it makes me think I believe it as long as it serves the big goal of keeping me far away from pain and rejection.

In school I claimed to not like team sports. My insecurities about not being wanted made me fear being picked last. The truth is, I love competition and probably would have been a great asset to any team I joined. I couldn't see it then.

As a young woman I claimed not to be looking for a commitment from the guys I met. My insecurities about not being lovable made me more comfortable with detached experience. Truthfully, I desperately wanted them to want me to be their girlfriend. My shit kept me from showing it.

I've lost track of the number of things I said I didn't care about in order to keep anyone from feeling sorry for me. Of all the risks I could take – the risk of being pitied was too terrible to face.

My Shit About Being A Heartless Monster

At nineteen, I had a one-night experience with a complete stranger. Completely out of character for me, to this day it feels like something that happened to someone else.

It was beautiful, really. Spontaneous. Sexy. It felt amazing to be wanted like that – and when it was all over, I ran like hell. The poor guy had to think I was a figment of his imagination, too.

Except our time together made a baby.

My father had passed away suddenly. I was young, broke, making six bucks an hour at work, living with roommates, and pregnant.

I fooled myself in a lot of ways about what I did and didn't want, but I knew I didn't want to be a burden on anyone and couldn't bear the thought of going on welfare. It seemed to me the worst possible life for a child.

I decided before I was halfway through the pregnancy to plan for adoption, worked with a private agency, chose parents, and waited for baby to come.

Two weeks after he was born, I melted into a puddle of tears and changed my mind. With help from my sister, I called the adoption off, picked up my son, and brought him home to her house.

Four months later, I was sharing a house with my cousin, doing my best to work and be a mom. In spite of my low pay, I didn't qualify for any assistance. I could get $44 a month in food stamps if I took one afternoon a month off to attend nutrition classes.

I never had enough money. I wrote a bad check to get baby formula and some-how avoided getting prosecuted for it. I couldn't pay my first babysitter on time so she fired me.

I left Frankie with my cousin after that and one day she showed up at work with him.

I turned around from my desk to see my baby in a dirty onesie, and my face flushed with embarrassment. My co-workers all came running to see him but I wanted to hide him from their sight. Who brings a dirty baby to visit an office? I felt sure everyone would think I was a terrible mother.

I grabbed him and ran into my boss's office, tears running down my face. I collapsed in a chair and held my son, feeling my heart break. I looked at my boss and said, "I've made a terrible mistake."

Everything I ever feared before he was born was coming true. I couldn't afford to take care of him. I couldn't pay for daycare. I couldn't pay for food. I had no options to change anything. We were alone and our lives would be one awful struggle after another.

"I wish I hadn't brought him home. I should have went through with the adoption."

In that moment I knew what I was going to do – and I did it.

Over the next twenty-four hours, I called the adoption agency, chose new parents, broke everyone's hearts, and handed my four-and-a-half-month-old baby over to a new family who desperately wanted him and could give him everything.

My sister was devastated by my choice. She held my son that last day, looked at me over his head, and told me that whatever success I built in my life, she'd never be able to forget what I gave up to get it.

Mostly, people were incredibly kind. The conversations about placing him for adoption were awkward and stilted. I felt judgment everywhere; whether it was really there or not didn't matter.

New shit ran and ran and ran...

- Only a heartless monster would give up her baby.
- She must not have loved him.
- What a selfish coward.
- She only cares about herself.
- What's wrong with her that she could do that?

My sister's painful words about never being able to celebrate anything good I accomplished rang in my ears when I took a promotion at work and later when I went back to school.

Years later she expressed regret and the words don't stand between us anymore. I realize she was only speaking what I was thinking. There are times when I wonder whether some of my self-sabotage in life has been related to feelings of guilt about "giving him up."

Some days I think a better version of myself would have kept him, gone on welfare, surrendered to a tough life of living in the system until he went to school full-time, then gone back to school myself and been one of those romantic hard luck stories, getting a degree and a wonderful job after all the years of struggle and suffering.

I love that kind of story. It speaks of passionate motherhood and winning over adversity.

When I dwell on that imaginary storyline, I get mired in shit. Why wasn't I like that? Why did I give up so easily? Did I not really love my son?

Ugh!!! Thinking about it still pulls all the right strings – but this is when I recognize my shit is at work and GET PAST IT!

I don't hold myself back from success anymore. I am not shy or reticent about sharing my story and my success with anyone. If I'm ever blessed to meet the grown man that is my first son, I would like him to be proud of the life I've built.

My Shit List Goes On

If these were my only sources of insecurity and fear, it'd be enough – but of course I have a whole list of shit I've let hold me back.

- I'm a high school dropout.
- I'm a college dropout too! Clearly a loser. A big fat quitter.
- I'm bossy. Nobody likes a bossy woman.
- I'm a know-it-all with a million opinions nobody wants to hear.
- I'm divorced and never remarried.
- I've been in debt most of my life and don't know how to manage money.
- Because I've mistreated my body, all of my health issues are my own fault. I deserve it.
- I can't keep up with others, nobody wants to do things with me. I'm a burden.

Given enough time, my shit list can fill pages.

Some shit is big and some shit is small.

Some shit requires a little side step to get past while others call for massive leaps of faith.

Writing this chapter, telling these stories... it's been emotional.

I've relived moments in my history, remembered the feelings, reviewed the beliefs, and brought to it the self-love I've adopted for myself in recent years.

It's been beautiful, really. It has put so much of my shit into perspective.

I'm so glad I don't let it hold me back anymore.

Kelly McCausey is a blogger/podcaster and business coach focused on content marketing and community building. She knows you want to publish content you're proud of for a community you love.

LovePeopleMakeMoney.com

CHAPTER TWO

Becoming Visible: The Power Of Story

Pam Hamilton

I'm nine years old, and I'm hanging out with my best friend in our afterschool program. We're laughing and joking and just having a good time.

Then here comes this guy. He's a fourth-grader, but he's in our program too. My friend starts talking to me about how cute he is, in the way third-grade girls talk about boys. And in that moment, I figure out — I really like girls. I know I'm not supposed to. I know I'm not supposed to like them as in, want to marry one; I'm only supposed to like boys that way.

Almost intuitively, at a deep gut level, I know I have to keep this to myself. It has to be my secret and I can't share it with anyone. I let my friend talk. I listen to her with my heart hurting, trying not to cry. And I feel very alone.

In that moment, I began to hide myself. Unconsciously, I began to create a story of me as a hideous person with an awful secret I had to shield from the world, and that if the true me was discovered, it would be disastrous. I became invisible.

Notice I didn't say anything about being gay. In 1969 I didn't know that word. I didn't know about lesbians or homosexuality or that there were other women in the world who felt like me. In fact, the infamous Stonewall Riots wouldn't happen until later, after school was over, in the summer of that year. And of course I wouldn't hear about them until much, much later. There was no newsreel footage, no mention of it on the 6:00 news. No, at nine years old, I thought I was the only girl in the world who liked other girls.

In between the bouts of loneliness that permeated my life because of the need to hide my secret, I had a great childhood. I played football and wrestled, endured stupid boys nicknaming me Harold, played tag and basketball, went fishing, swimming, biking and hiking, climbed trees, caught and released hundreds of fireflies, and found all kinds of stray animals I brought home to care for.

And I alternately prayed to either start liking boys the way my girl-friends did, or tried to kiss my elbow so that I would turn into a boy and it would be okay to like girls like my boy-friends did. I didn't really want to be a boy, but to my nine-year-old mind, it was a small price to pay to get to kiss girls.

Keeping My Secret

I kept my secret, or at least I thought I did. I didn't tell anyone. I even pretended to like boys. And I officially became a member of my church and sang in the choir. By junior high school I had mostly mastered the art of being invisible. I vividly remember sitting in the back corner of my homeroom class in my puffy brown coat, head down, willing the teacher not to see me for any reason.

I had learned that there were men who liked other men. My mother had hired an openly gay man to work at her company that she operated from the first floor of our home. He was very clear with the women who tried to flirt with him that he liked men. I had overheard him say it at least twice. I finally broke down and asked my uncle about it. It was easy to talk with him about almost anything.

"Everyone likes men, so there's all kinds of possibilities to hookup," he had said.

"What about girls?" I asked, very carefully. "Everybody likes women too," I finished off lamely. But my uncle assured me that it wasn't like that for women. Men were just sexual, and some men didn't have any control and experimented with perversions, he told me. That's why the Bible only spoke about men lying down with other men, I thought. My Pastor called men who did that "Abominations unto the Lord."

I had given up on trying to kiss my elbow as hopeless. But I continued to pray daily, almost feverishly, every time I found another woman/girl attractive — especially at church.

But despite my attempts to keep my secret, I think my mom knew, and she loved me anyway. My mom would always say "Pam and the boys," meaning my younger brothers, and she called my sisters the girls. She bought dolls and dollhouses for the girls, but not for me. Not even once. The boys and I got karate and kung-fu lessons, and 10-speed bicycles to race around town on.

And when I was older, my mom had hired that openly gay man to work at her company. I think she wanted me to know it was okay. But in my mind, I desperately needed to keep my secret because all of the people I loved would despise and disown me. And my story kept me invisible and in pain. I never saw those overtures, except in hindsight years later.

When I was growing up it was illegal for adults to talk to kids about stuff like being gay, having an abortion if they were pregnant, or even using condoms so they wouldn't get pregnant. They could be arrested and fined for perverting a minor. We had sex-ed class where they talked about "reproductive organs," marriage, and the procreative process.

So it was a true blessing to me that we lived next door to a woman named Lavender. That's not her real name, but it'll have to do for this story. Lavender was a heavy-set woman who happened to be a prostitute. She was also a staunch protector of kids and the downtrodden. Everyone loved Lavender, even the church-going folks. She often had the courage to do what others wouldn't, even though they wanted to. I learned to confront child abusers and bullies head-on from Lavender, who often did just that in my neighborhood.

When I would get off the train at night coming home late from a theatre job or a martial arts lesson, both me and my mom counted on the fact that Lavender would be on her street corner when I popped out of the train station. She and I would wave to each other and she would keep her eye on me as I walked home as quickly as I could.

Lavender was the first person who spoke to me about being "queer," as she called it. I was walking home feeling particularly glum. I was a senior in high school and the neighborhood boys were being jerks regularly now. They didn't want me to play basketball or football or baseball with them anymore and they were pissed that I could still beat most of them up if they messed with me. They wanted me to act like a girl and have a boyfriend and braid his hair. I had beaten my last one up for threatening me when I didn't want to have sex with him. So I wasn't acting right at all in their minds.

Lavender was sitting on her stoop as I trooped up the block. She called me over to talk. I sat next to her and complained about the situation with the boys. "Oh, they're just mad cause you're getting more pussy than they are!" she exclaimed casually. I did a double take. My first thought was, *I wish I was!* My second thought was, *Wait. How did she even know I wanted to be with girls?!*

The look on my face must have made her have second thoughts. "I mean, you're queer, right?" she asked me. I looked at her blank for a moment, and then before she could stop talking to me altogether, I blurted out, "Girls can be queer?"

I had heard the term in high school, usually in a derogatory manner aimed at a particular male dancer who folks had decided was too effeminate. She smiled at me and said yes, girls can be queer.

"They're called lesbians," she told me. "You can find books about it at the library." I thanked her and made a mental note to head to the library as soon as possible.

I was a regular at most of the libraries within easy travel distance from my house or school. I went every week or two and got a stack of books to read, and it was my refuge when I decided to play hooky from school or just needed a break from everything. So when I went to my local library to ask about a book on lesbians, the librarian was shocked. She tried to hide it as she asked me, "Why would you want a book like that?!" But I heard the shock and dismay anyway.

I quickly explained that I had to do a report for my social studies class at school. It was true. I had found out I had to do a report the day after speaking with Lavender and had immediately chosen that topic. The librarian, satisfied with my explanation, gave me three books, and one of them lead me to a church that was led by a lesbian pastor. It was, in retrospect, the beginning of my journey to visibility.

I was born in February. That meant I turned a year older halfway through the school year, which turned out to be very fortunate for me my senior year. I was eighteen when I went to see the lesbian pastor. It meant she could talk to me. And I could go to church there, where I was assured that God still loved me, even if I was gay. I just did it all in secret.

I didn't tell my mom, who went to church elsewhere, that I had quit my old church; I just stopped going. I listened to the choir and sermon on the radio on Sundays but I didn't go. The final straw had come as the church was organizing a rally against the policies of our mayor. As we were preparing for the rally, our pastor had said, "This man doesn't even deserve to be mayor, he's a flaming faggot!"

I could see the vein pulsing on the side of his neck, feel his anger. My face flushed, and I was glad I was Black and no one would see my discomfort and embarrassment. Although there were many reasons our mayor needed to step down, none of them had anything to do with his sexual orientation. I wasn't even sure that he was gay. But I was sure that I couldn't worship in a place where the leader would hate me that much if he ever learned my secret.

When I found the new church, the church where God loved me no matter what, I started attending again. I never said it wasn't my old church. I just said "church." I let people make their own assumptions. I trusted God would understand, but everyone else... that part I wasn't even almost sure of.

The Plan

I finally had a name for what I was, and I celebrated that I wasn't the only one. Although being gay was definitely frowned upon, I didn't want to keep my secret anymore. And I hatched a plan for coming out to my family. But first, I would go to college far away and make sure I could survive if they stopped loving me.

I moved from New York City to California to attend college. My mom accompanied me to help me get settled in for my first year. It felt like a special retreat, just me and my mom hanging out, without my brothers and sisters and cousins and her job interfering.

But the time came to an end all too swiftly. As she got into the shuttle bus heading back to the airport, we both looked at each other. It hit us like a Mack truck: "She's leaving me here!" We both tried not to cry. I would get to call home at the end of the week, on Sunday. My big plan had been to stay in California at the end of my first year, to stay away from family. Now I wondered if I'd even survive until Sunday.

I decided I would make the most of the opportunity to explore my new freedom but slowly, carefully. I tried to connect to other women like me — women who love women.

It was the late '70s, and it was still unacceptable and often dangerous to be gay. There were a few defiant heroes who were openly gay, and I was hoping to find some of those women who would out themselves and put their lives on the line while I stayed hidden. I didn't think of it that way at the time. But I was looking for these women who'd be in plain sight while I stayed safe behind my wall of invisibility.

It took a long time before I found a woman who was openly bisexual. All we really had in common was that we both liked women and loved theatre and art, but we slowly built a friendship anyway. It was disappointing, and not at all what I had hoped for. I missed my friends in NYC. The lesbian pastor's daughter, who was really cute and really into me but totally off limits, wrote me weekly letters scented with her perfume. She was oblivious to her Mom's determination to raise a straight daughter. And I dreamed of being home.

When my mom called at the end of the school year to say she was making arrangements for me to fly home, I told her I was going to stay in California that summer. My heart was breaking as I said it.

She demanded to know why. I was petrified. I had already lost friends my senior year of high school. I had friends who had lost family since I had come to college. I bit the bullet anyway and told her. My mom assured me that home was my safe space.

"I can't protect you from the world," she said. "But no one is going to bother you in this house." So I went home. But I understood, it was only safe in my house. Not out in the world.

By my second year I'd come out to a few close friends and immediate family members and was a little less invisible. But the battle scars were still there. I worked hard to stay under the radar. My life was haunted by self-doubt and loathing, low self-esteem, and fear of almost everything.

I was crawling out of my shell, but gun-shy just the same. There was a young woman I liked, a violinist. I attended all of her concerts and even her rehearsals when I could. I thought she was brilliant. She invited me to Jamaica to spend the holiday with her and her family.

I gathered up my wits about me and wrote her a poem. I misread the signs. I was disinvited to Jamaica, to her rehearsals, to her concerts, to her life. She told everyone at school... I was exiled.

I had let my secret slip and was facing the consequences. I felt like some grotesque, unlovable freak of nature. The words of my former pastor rang in my ears: homosexuality is an abomination before the Lord. I had forgotten to be invisible.

I wanted to be dead. My story that started when I was nine years old was reinforced. I got better at functioning in the world while being invisible. But I was in pain. And I was eating my pain.

I switched colleges for my junior year to escape the accusing stares of former friends and found other women like me. And I finally had a girlfriend! We joined the feminist movement and the gay movement together — "Silence = Death," I shouted into the megaphone at the protests and the parades, and the hallowed grounds of my college campus, but not in my neighborhood, not yet. In my neighborhood I was stealth and silent, like a ninja.

I survived and finally graduated. And a few years later I met the woman who would eventually become my wife. But I stayed under the radar. I was working, but not living up to my potential. I was afraid in the real world; my secret had me more bound up than ever. Only the people closest to me knew. I'd stopped trying to be straight, but I was still hiding and using food to numb the pain, and it was making me sick inside. I needed to prove that my former pastor was wrong, that I wasn't an abomination in God's eyes, not a mistake. That I was worthy of respect and love.

Awakening & Yearnings

I went to law school, graduated, and prepared to take the bar exam. After months of studying I finally felt like maybe I was prepared.

The night before the examination I decided to get to bed early. But I ended up tossing and turning. I was dreaming, and in the dream I was running, and my friends were running too. We had scattered in different directions as bullets whizzed all around us, and then I was floating.

I was in a room with shimmering walls illuminated by a soft light that seemed not to have a source. I rubbed my eyes, even in the dream, thinking they were playing tricks on me. Then my uncle came into the room. In the dream I accepted this as normal. But my uncle had passed years earlier. "Death is an illusion," he said. "We never really die." He faded from view even as he finished the sentence.

Then a friend from my theatre days, a choreographer and dancer who had also passed away, appeared. "Death is an illusion," he said, echoing my uncle. "It's like a chess game — with every move you learn something new." As he faded away, I started wondering why dead people were disturbing my sleep to talk to me about death. Then the phone rang, and I was awake.

One of my brothers was on the phone. He told me our youngest brother had been shot in the head. I took the news like, "Okay, so where is he now?" We knew lots of folks who had gotten shot, even in the head. It was everyday news in the part of Brooklyn where we lived. It wasn't called "Do or Die BedSty" for nothing.

Except my little brother didn't make it. He had been shot down in the street as he and his friends were fleeing for their lives, running from a group of guys who had opened fire to defend their leader's right to be with a girl who didn't want to be with him.

I hung up the phone and looked at the clock. It was 3:00 in the morning. I called my sister and her husband answered. My call meant the news she had received a few minutes earlier was real. She was in shock and couldn't talk.

As I placed the phone on the receiver, my mom called. She said she was coming to get me. She and my step-dad needed to hold onto someone, they needed help making calls, they just needed... something. Their baby was gone, he had just turned seventeen, and we were going to have to put him in the ground. My wife helped me get dressed, my mind too numb to move my hands.

My bar examination was scheduled to start at 8:00 that morning. I had been up all night calling the rest of the family and trying to give some form of comfort to my mom and dad; mostly, I just held a safe space for them to cry. But as daylight slowly crept up on the city and siblings arrived at the house, folks remembered I was supposed to be taking the bar exam. They remembered that I would have to wait another year to take it again. And they remembered how much I had sacrificed to get to that point. They insisted I go take my exam.

My wife drove me through the deserted city streets to the enormous Jacob Javits Center in Manhattan where the exam was being held. She promised to bring me lunch at the break and to keep in touch with the family. And off I went, delirious from lack of sleep and the pain of losing a loved one. I remember looking at my exam paper shortly before the morning session ended and seeing answer after answer completed that I didn't remember filling in.

Months later, I learned that I had passed. It was a miracle; I don't know how I did it. And as I was being sworn in almost a year later, I wished I could shout out to the rooftops how happy I was, finally. I had a great job, a loving wife, and a son on the way.

But I was still invisible in most circles. Invisibility had become a habit that was hard to break. Every time I made a little headway, something would happen to remind me of the consequences of being visible. My story would be reinforced: I was a hideous person with an awful secret and it would be disastrous if the true me was discovered.

I was battling an internal struggle of epic proportions. I wanted to be successful, to have my own business, to live the kind of life I imagined for myself, to be able to provide for my little family. But I was failing at it... over and over again.

I set goals, S.M.A.R.T goals... I visualized, and I worked hard. Yet in the end, I always found a way to sabotage my efforts and pull myself back down to nothing — because the success I dreamed of went against my prime directive, which was to be invisible. I couldn't be invisible and have the success I wanted. I needed to change my story of me, so I could become the me I wanted to be, the me that could own the success I dreamed of.

Then Ellen DeGeneres came out on national TV and the world didn't stop.

Afraid, but hopeful, I asked God to help me. I wanted to confirm that I was not a mistake, not an abomination. I wanted to raise my son and not be invisible. And God answered in a dream!

In the dream I am with my wife. We are in a small village in a little hut. It has openings for windows and doors, but there is no glass, no doors, just openings.

We are sitting together on the dirt floor in the middle of the room. There are people outside surrounding the hut. They are shouting and yelling and condemning us. They throw stones and sticks. For the first time, in an uncharacteristic show of self-love, I decide to stand up for myself. I stand up and walk to the open doorway to confront them. But they are all ME. I'm in shock. I look at the faces of each agitator and as I do, they stop and look back at me. My face on every one of them.

That was my breakthrough moment. I realized that I was the real judge, jury, and executioner. I was creating the world that kept me small and afraid, and more importantly... I could change it.

I wish I could say that my life changed for the better immediately. But that would be a lie. Understanding something, even on a gut level, is not the same as living it. I still had to learn to walk the talk. And it shook my life to the core.

I tried to fill three high-level positions at work while being a parent and a wife and building my own business on the side. I did that last part without my wife's consent or support. I worked weekends and my wife went out dancing with friends because I was too tired to.

We argued a lot. Between that and the pressure of her family's disapproval of her lifestyle, she said she wanted to leave me, and I didn't fight it. I let her go because I loved her, but in hindsight, I realize it may not have felt like that to her.

I was exhausted and my health was declining as I went through the emotional upheaval of a divorce and tried to negotiate a way to stay in my son's life when I had no legal rights to lean on... and look for a new place to live in an overpriced housing market.

I made mistakes and they cost me dearly. I lost my job, my wife, and even my health as I struggled to create the life I desired.

But I now knew that I created my own reality. I began to see the connecting dots. I finally understood that I was Soul and that I existed because God loved me, right then as I was and right now, as I am. For the first time, I was free and filled with gratitude and joy. I finally got it. Now, I needed to do something with it, manifest it. But what was the reality I wanted to create?

Breakthroughs & Transformation

I was a lawyer and being paid well, but I wasn't happy with the job. I was frustrated at not being able to truly help my clients so I left that job for a lower-paying, hopefully more fulfilling job. I had more prestige as general counsel. But it still didn't resonate.

I began to listen. Really listen to the words I was saying to myself, the thoughts running through my head. I started to see how my negative self-talk, the thoughts and stories I told myself on a daily basis, impacted the successes I hoped to achieve.

I began to understand that my mind was not my friend. But it could be a powerful tool if I took control over it. I started practicing simple tools to change my thoughts and convert my negative self-talk to more neutral, if not positive, language; and then, slowly, more positive-leaning.

When I finally gathered the courage to look inside myself – I found wisdom, love, inner strength, and courage. And I finally understood, I have always been this person. I have always been enough from the moment I was born. It was only my stories that separated me from this truth.

Then one day I saw Oprah Winfrey doing her last TV show on ABC. She stood on a bare stage and just talked to her audience from her heart. She said she's always believed herself to be a teacher. Not the kind that stands in front of a classroom and teaches rote lessons, but a teacher of transformation and change. And in that instant, I knew what I wanted to do. I knew I was that, too: a teacher, a coach. I wanted to help aspiring entrepreneurs learn to stop playing small, to learn to step into a larger room, find their passion, and live the life they've imagined.

Living The Dream

That's why I was so frustrated with my previous jobs — I was never able to help my clients reach their full potential. I wasn't living my own potential. I saw the mountaintop.

My life had been shaken to the core, but it proved to be a blessing in disguise. I got coached and I came out of it a whole person.

I began working with small business owners and aspiring entrepreneurs all over the state of New York, helping them step into their true calling and build the business of their dreams. Soon I would spread out to the whole country and become a published author. I've spoken on multiple stages and been hired by the SBA's Small Business Development Center to present at workshops and trainings.

But it's not just my financial and business life that changed. I have a wife who loves me and a great relationship with my son. Even my family relationships have changed. My parents and siblings see me as a whole and loving person. I have friends and finally, I am no longer invisible. I am alive and loved and I share that love with everyone who crosses my path.

Here's the big takeaway: I was never an abomination, and I was always loved. It was the stories I told myself that made me invisible and afraid. I was the one guarding all the doors and holding all the keys. I was the only one really standing in my way. And learning to get out of my way, to change the stories I told myself, changed everything.

I became visible in my life and in my business, and it mattered. No matter what stories you are telling yourself right now, no matter what things you have ingrained into your psyche based on what others have said to you or about you, you are enough too.

Your talents, skills and knowledge are your God-given gifts to share with the world. It's the stories we tell ourselves that keep us stuck and afraid, struggling and playing small. But we can flip the script; we can make a conscious choice to change our narrative and truly live the life we want. We can be paid well and make a positive impact in the world sharing our gifts through a business we love.

I believe everyone has a dream about who or what they want to be. And each of us has the ability to achieve it, if we would just get out of our own way.

Pam Hamilton is an attorney and business coach who is passionate about helping small business owners get past their "stuff" and grow thriving businesses that create wealth and make a positive impact in the world.

BuildingVisibility.com

CHAPTER THREE

Letting Go Of What Doesn't Matter

Lady Rayven Monique

I nearly manifested my own death. Truly, I spoke it into existence.

"When I die," I'd say, "I want to hemorrhage because it's so easy and so peaceful."

I said this repeatedly over the course of a decade.

When I die, I want to hemorrhage.

Why would anyone say such a thing?

Because I had been there once. In 2005, as a surrogate to twins, I hemorrhaged during delivery and needed three blood transfusions. And the thing I remembered most was how peaceful everything was. The whole place could have been burning down around me and I wouldn't have cared. It was relaxing. Painless.

That's it, I decided: When I die, I want to hemorrhage. I said it lots and lots and lots of times, without much thought.

The universe listens even when we don't.

Thirteen years later, I was in a panic over money... again. This was a pattern throughout my life. I'd be great at manifesting all kinds of things — the perfect man, trips, you name it — but the sticking point was always money.

The story I made up was that I could pull money out of my ass when I needed it. And of course, that's always how it happened. Reach the end, completely freak out, money would show up. Smooth cash flow? That wasn't part of my story.

So this was the latest freak-out, and it was a big one: I had invested more than $100,000 into a business idea that was failing. I found myself six figures in debt with no income and thousands a month in carrying costs.

In desperation, I turned to the one idea that had always worked: surrogacy. I was good at it, my body normally handled it well, and I had delivered seven babies already (in addition to two of my own). I'd been through it so many times, I knew what to expect.

One last time, just to make ends meet. Business decision.

In that panic, I was doing something I counsel 100 percent of women considering surrogacy NOT to do: choosing it for the money.

The problem was, I didn't really want to do it. I had declared myself finished, and by making a decision rooted in desperation, I went into it with resistance.

My subconscious knew the truth.

I don't want to do another surrogacy. I don't want to do another surrogacy.

The universe listens.

I signed up for another surrogacy and was matched within six months. Babies ten and eleven were soon on the way.

Something's Different This Time

I've always carried babies to term — in fact, I usually needed to be induced at forty weeks, even with twins (which I've carried three times).

So when my water broke at thirty weeks, I was surprised.

The doctors kept me in the hospital on bed rest and I rested five days before my body went into labor. I delivered both babies — each healthy, but small — without a C-section, though the placenta had to be surgically removed. I went home two days later.

Something was different.

Every other time, I'd needed no recovery time. This time I was tired, I wasn't hungry, and my mom and boyfriend were forcing me to eat. I had the shakes. My temperature would climb to 104, the shakes would start, and I'd cycle through again and again. I wound up in and out of the emergency room four times, with ultrasounds and other tests failing to find anything wrong.

For ER visit #2, my lungs were congested and I was admitted for two days while they did a CAT scan and an echocardiogram and drained fluid from my lungs. I was still sick but nothing showed up on the tests.

A few days later, I started to hemorrhage: ER visit #3. The doctors hypothesized that some of the placenta was still inside, and they gave me meds to get rid of it.

I went home with my boyfriend and mother. Before going to bed, I turned to my boyfriend and gave him instructions.

"This is going to sound strange," I said, "but if I do anything weird, pull the sheets back and check."

At midnight, I took a contraction pill and an Oxycontin and went to bed.

An hour later, I woke up in the worst pain I've ever been in. Having taken the painkiller just an hour earlier, I knew I couldn't have more of that. A bottle of ibuprofen sat on the nightstand next to my bed yet, despite it being an arm's length away, I couldn't reach over and get it. I sat in bed for ten minutes debating what to do. Finally, I woke up my boyfriend and asked him to get the ibuprofen for me.

Groggy, he got up and started over to my side of the bed before it dawned on him: *This is weird. She should be able to reach the bottle.* He pulled the bedsheet off of me.

I was covered with blood.

He grabbed the phone and was calling an ambulance when my mother, a nurse, came in. She took one look at me and passed out. (My boyfriend half-jokingly wondered aloud whether he should call one ambulance or two.)

This was ER trip #4. My blood pressure was 30/60 and it took about 45 minutes to get to the hospital. I was in excruciating pain but they couldn't give me pain medication because my blood pressure was too low.

Three Rooms

We were at the bustling emergency room when in the midst of the chaos, I suddenly saw three rooms appear in front of me.

"Mom," I said, "there are these rooms here."

My mother had experienced people near death talking like this before.

"Rayven," she answered, trying to stay calm, "Stay in this room."

I could see everything, the hospital bed and the staff hard at work around me. And I could also see the rooms, or at least the doors to them.

The pain had gone to one room. Its door was closed and cool; pain would not be a part of this decision.

The doors to the other two rooms were open. Each was equally warm and inviting. The one to my left was Here and the one in the center was Beyond.

I had a choice: walk through one or the other. Stay here in this existence or go on. And the choice was as simple as choosing whether to wear my sneakers or my boots. It didn't feel life-altering and it didn't feel as though I should charge it with emotion. It didn't feel hard at all. It was easy to stay, and it would have been just as easy to go.

I didn't think about what would happen if I left, about whether my boyfriend, mom, and children would be sad. There was no good, bad, right or wrong, no consequences to either decision. No should. It was simply, "Which do you want?"

I could go either way.

Then a feeling bubbled up.

Oh Hell, no.

Days earlier, my son had moved out of the house. As much as I loved him, I was finally an empty nester, something I had looked forward to for 18 years. There were so many things I wanted to do in life, and I had been waiting for my kids to grow up to do them.

I am not gonna walk away now, as it's just beginning.

That was it.

I chose to stay.

Clarity Arrives

During that pregnancy and delivery, I had experienced a freak occurrence, placenta accreta, a condition in which the placenta attaches too deeply to the uterine wall. The condition is usually discovered during an ultrasound but in my case, it had attached in the curve of the uterus and no one had seen it.

I needed eight blood transfusions, another D&C (dilation and curettage, a procedure to remove tissue from inside the uterus), and a hysterectomy.

A hysterectomy...

I don't want to do another surrogacy.

The universe listens.

This time, I listened too. When facing those rooms, I came to a sudden realization: all of the things I thought mattered in life — none of it mattered. I could let it all go. Pay the bills or don't pay the bills. I'm still going to be able to do the things I want to do.

I asked myself what I wanted, and I didn't get caught up in how it would happen. International travel, the home of my dreams; money is required, but I wouldn't worry about it. I got really clear about the things I was putting off until the days I had money. Instead of declining, I signed up and believed. Really believed.

I recognized that the way I *think* I'm going to get from A to Z is not necessarily how it's going to turn out. I also recognized that none of us really owns anything.

In the year after that incident, I moved into my dream house with five acres in the country and started remodeling the home. I'm getting to be a steward of the land I want. I'm going for the experience and the emotion of it, and I'm getting that.

I traveled to the UK and visited Stonehenge. I made plans to spend six weeks in Europe with my best friend and to visit Croatia.

I invested money in yoga teacher training. I also want to be a master herbalist, which is a serious hobby but not a money-making venture. Mornings are spent doing things I love: yoga, meditation, my daily desires for the day, time on hobbies.

I haven't paid off the debt yet, but I've figured out how to chip away at that and pay myself also.

I still work, I still set goals, I still make business plans. But the obsession is gone. It's about taking action and letting go of having to know exactly how it will work out.

I went from, "I can't do that now" to "This is the result I want; I'm going to work towards that, and everything else works itself out along the way."

And that's not to say the stress never shows up. I do occasionally find myself back in the habit of freaking out. It wasn't like a switch got flipped and it's never going to happen again; we're human and our brains work in a certain way. Now, however, I recognize what's happening. It's "Oh shit, I'm doing that again; let's not do that again." And I bring myself back to focusing on the end result.

It wasn't part of my plan to share my story or create retreats or coach people on the Law of Attraction. It just so happened that I kept taking the next step, and then the next step to take would open up.

I hosted my first retreat on an off-the-cuff dare from a friend. I started a podcast, private coaching, and developed a new website. It's been one thing after another.

Today I'm a happiness and abundance coach who shows people how to get what they want in life. I encourage people to live life on their own terms.

And I have no idea where this is going to end. I don't have to know what it's going to look like.

I'm just taking steps.

Lady Rayven Monique is a doer in life - she does things that others can't or won't. A true original, Rayven believes that happiness is our natural state of being, and guides others to manifesting their own dreams.

Abundability.com

CHAPTER FOUR

From Yes To Yes

Lane Therrell

My Yes Was My Bond

On Christmas morning in 1995, I stood shivering in my bathrobe in the back yard. I was turning over frost-encrusted flower pots, looking for the next note in the scavenger hunt my boyfriend had set up as a way of delivering my Christmas gift. I glanced over at him. He stood with his fists clasped at his sides, quivering with excitement — or possibly cold — a gleeful boyish grin on his face.

I was annoyed. The scavenger hunt had started out as a fun idea, but it had dragged on for far too long. We'd been at it for an hour now; I'd collected eight notes so far, and there was no end in sight. It was cold outside! Enough was enough.

As I paused to stretch my back and rub my arms for warmth, I felt an intense gaze from my boyfriend's close-set, too-blue eyes. My annoyance faded a bit. I had a soft spot for this man. I felt protective towards him. He had not had a stable childhood like mine. Someone needed to give him a chance. Why not me?

I returned to my task while trying not to get my robe dirty. Under the next clay pot was a handwritten note: *Look in the kitchen cabinet.*

We trooped back into the blessed warmth of the kitchen. I surveyed the long row of cabinets over the sink, and he stood there with the same gleeful grin on his face. My annoyance began creeping back.

"We could speed this up if you tell me which cabinet to look in," I said in an even tone, trying not to let my annoyance show. He tilted his head to indicate the cabinet closest to the refrigerator.

The open cabinet revealed a solitary box of Wheaties cereal with a yellow Post-It note: Open me.

I took the box of cereal off the shelf and shook it while I asked, "Breakfast?"

"Sure," he grinned. "I'll grab the milk."

A small blue box tumbled out into the white Corian bowl amid the cascade of cereal flakes.

"Is this what I've been looking for?" I plucked the box out of the pile of dry cereal and held it up between my right thumb and forefinger next to my face. In an effort to counter my baseline annoyance with levity, I smiled broadly, and made a Vanna White gesture with my left hand underneath the box.

"Your Christmas present," he announced in his best game show host voice.

I lifted the hinged lid on the blue box and caught my breath as a diamond ring sparkled up at me. I felt a pang of guilt that I hadn't seen this coming. I had gotten him a sweater for Christmas, and the disparity between our gifts was clear.

"What's this?"

"It's how much I love you," he said. "Will you marry me?"

I held the surprisingly heavy gold ring up to the light before trying it on. The morning light danced with miniature rainbows through ten diamonds in a shared prong setting. The antique ring, which he'd bought at an auction, was far too large for me and it was engraved with someone else's name and anniversary date. But my boyfriend had just said he loved me and had asked me to marry him.

Tears of what I interpreted as joy blurred my vision as I slipped the too-large ring onto the middle finger of my right hand, where it came closest to fitting. I extended my hand so he could see.

Instead of looking at the ring, he grabbed my hand and pulled me close, wrapping his long arms around me in a crushing hug. "Well what do you say?" he asked in a too-loud voice. I nodded affirmatively and mumbled "yes" into his shoulder. My mind raced to find a way to gracefully exit his overly enthusiastic bearhug, which was at once suffocating and bruising. I tapped his bulging bicep to get him to release the embrace.

I was in a daze. I had just said yes to a proposal of marriage. This life-changing moment had snuck up on me like a ninja in the night. And it was over far too quickly. I understood then that the hour-long scavenger hunt had been his valiant attempt at trying to make the moment last. And I had been annoyed the whole time! A wave of shame washed over me.

This proposal and acceptance was not the romantic moment I had always imagined: My fingernails were dirty with garden soil, I was shivering in my bathrobe, there were Wheaties flakes all over the countertop, and I felt crushed under the weight of an overly enthusiastic hug from my now-fiancé. Yet, no one outside my family of origin had ever told me they loved me. These were words I had always longed to hear. My boyfriend had given me a beautiful gift, and he had asked me the question of a lifetime. It never occurred to me that there was any answer to his question other than *yes*.

The Yes I Was Born With

I grew up in Charlotte, North Carolina, in the early 1970s. It's a big city now, but in those days my family's small corner of the South retained a genuine small-town feel. My parents grew up in the same local area where I was born and raised. And I went all the way through public school, K-12, with the same group of peers, mostly the children of my parents' former classmates.

I was a sheltered child who never learned "street-smarts." In our suburban/ rural neighborhood there were no streets or sidewalks to play on. We had back yards instead. And there were plenty of safe woods to play in too, which suited my introverted, natural-science-geek preferences just fine. My idea of a good time was riding my horse through the woods, drawing pictures, and puttering in the garden. I thrived in this insular environment.

As socially sheltered as my childhood was, my upbringing was intellectually expansive. Both of my parents were teachers, so everything in our lives was a teachable moment. Outdoor adventures and interactions with animals of all species were highly encouraged. Every aspect of daily life had the potential to become a science experiment or a craft project. But this idyllic emphasis on creative and intellectual pursuit was built upon a rigid structure. Rules and manners were strictly enforced by regular church attendance and a sea of elderly relatives and neighbors.

No "bad words" were allowed in my vocabulary. Even "darn" was forbidden. "Please" and "thank you" were mandatory in every requested transaction. And a simple "yes," or "no" was never sufficient. It always had to be followed by a show of respect or gratitude — as in, "Yes Sir," "Yes Ma'am," or "No thank you." Constant corrections drilled these communication parameters into my head.

The topics of conversation around our family dinner table were more often ideas and concepts rather than people and their behaviors. Drama, manipulation, and gamesmanship were not part of my experience. The closest I got to strategy was watching Perry Mason reruns. The lessons I learned about relationships and human interaction stemmed from these gems: Obey God and your elders (in that order), and your word is your bond. In the world of my childhood, "yes" formed a non-negotiable contract with no possibility for revisions or amendments.

I didn't figure it out until later in life, but the culture of the South, at least for female children, was all about meeting expectations and pleasing others. There was an undercurrent of ironclad rigidity that flowed beneath the surface. Complying with the polite Bible Belt culture made me into a subservient dishrag. It was subtle, but there was an element of entrapment and victimization at play in my life from the beginning.

What Is Yes, Anyway?

Let's pause for a moment and unpack the idea of yes. Yes is a vast concept, multifaceted and all-encompassing. Too often, we take "yes" for granted. Saying yes involves consent. Acceptance. Commitment. It's a type of affirmation. And it can become a trap or a false identity if you're not clear about your boundaries.

There was a sincere commitment that went along with that proposal of marriage I accepted back in 1995. From the moment I said yes, it was as if I had already said the ceremonial "I Do." So during the course of the relationship, whenever things got violent or abusive, I relied on my commitment, my "yes," as my strength. It became a justification for staying in the relationship. This was an example of the yes working against me — it trapped me in the bad relationship.

Discovering that it was possible to break the sacred contract was a key turning point for me.

The Unrequited Yes

Fast forward five years and six months after the scavenger hunt.

By this time, our wedding date had become a moving target. It had been set and re-set so many times I couldn't count them all. There was always a rationale, a parade of excuses – each of which sounded plausible at the time: Let's buy a house first. Let's save more so we can have a bigger reception. Let's wait until you're settled in at your new job.

The excuses always came from him, but I went along with them. And because

I was loyal, because I had said yes to what was to me an ironclad commitment, I stayed in the relationship.

And then one warm June afternoon, the FBI showed up at my house.

I went outside to water the marigolds that lined the driveway, and was surprised to see a man in a dark suit walking towards me. I hadn't heard him drive up.

"Miss Therrell, Miss Therrell. Are you Miss Therrell?"

This young man did not look familiar to me. How did he know my name? Had I attended college with him? Why was he dressed in a suit on such a hot day?

"Do I know you?"

"I'm agent Smith. I'm with the FBI." He flashed his badge just like they do in the movies. "I need to ask you a few questions."

"Sure. What about?"

Agent Smith rattled off a long list of names of famous artists — artists whose paintings I had heard my fiancé talk about as they pertained to his work, which he described as "authenticating" artwork as investments for his clients. I never asked him about his work. I wasn't interested, quite frankly. My own job with a small but busy public relations firm was stressful enough.

The agent's words blurred together in a monolithic tower of babble. I didn't fully comprehend what he was talking about, but I was able to pick out words and phrases, like "eBay," "shill bidding," and "wire fraud," which did not sound positive.

Slowly, I began making connections. My fiancé had recently started selling paintings directly to customers through a new online auction service called eBay. I had set him up with an account using my credit card so he could experiment with it. Although I had no idea what shill bidding or wire fraud were, I reasoned they must have something to do with this Internet auction site. It began to dawn on me that the agent was telling me that something illegal was happening on eBay, and the FBI (the FBI!) thought I was the one who was doing it.

I realized Agent Smith had stopped talking and was waiting for me to respond.

"It sounds to me like you need to speak with my fiancé. He's the one who uses the eBay account you're talking about."

"Where is he? May I speak with him?"

"He's not here right now."

The agent sized me up and almost inaudibly said, "Of course he's not." In a much more audible, professional tone, he added, "Well, you need to come with me for further questioning."

"Am I being arrested?" I asked, suddenly panicked.

"No. We just need you to answer some more questions."

"Well, it sounds to me like I need a lawyer. I'm not going anywhere with you without a lawyer present."

The agent pursed his lips and took a deep breath that was released in a heavy sigh. He handed me his business card. "Call us as soon as you have your lawyer. You have twenty-four hours."

I accepted the card with trembling fingers. I broke out in a cold sweat as I stood in the blazing sun watching him return to his car and drive down the driveway.

Twenty-four hours? That meant I needed a lawyer by this time tomorrow.

I went back inside the house. As soon as I closed the door behind me, I began shaking uncontrollably. My heart was beating too fast and I had trouble catching my breath. I felt dizzy and the room began spinning. I vomited in the sink, and afterwards I felt like I had stepped into an animated cartoon: Nothing seemed or felt familiar or real. My thoughts were racing. I sat down at the kitchen table and a thought from somewhere else in my mind seemed to say, "Get a grip!"

In that moment, I opened the local phone book and turned to the yellow pages under the listings for criminal lawyers. It was after 5:00 p.m., but I started at the top of the list and began calling. I called office after office, willing someone to pick up. Finally, someone did.

"Law offices. Can I help you?"

"Yes, please, I sure hope so. I'm being accused of wire fraud—by the FBI. I didn't do it, but it seems I'm in urgent need of a lawyer."

"That's what we're here for. Can you give me a brief summary of what happened?"

I told my story and made an appointment for myself and my fiancé for 2 p.m. the next afternoon.

Then I called my fiancé to let him know.

"You'll never guess who was just here."

"Who?"

"The FBI."

"What?"

"Yep. They named a bunch of artists and talked about eBay and shill bidding and wire fraud. It didn't make any sense to me, and I have no idea what's going on, but evidently some mistakes have been made using that eBay account I set up for you. The account is in my name, so they think I'm doing it — whatever 'it' is. They wanted to take me away today."

Silence.

"Are you there?"

"Yes. You didn't go anywhere with them, did you?"

"No. I told them I needed a lawyer. He said I had twenty-four hours to find one. But it sounds to me like you're the one who needs the lawyer. I have no idea what's going on. But something's not right here, and it needs to get straightened out. I made an appointment with a lawyer for us both tomorrow afternoon. It's at 2 p.m. Here's the address. Don't be late."

The next day, at 1:59 p.m., I was sitting at a big wooden desk across from a man in an expensive-looking suit. When the clock on the wall struck 2 p.m., the lawyer checked his wristwatch. "This fiancé of yours, is he usually on time?"

"Yes, sir. He said he'd be here."

"Well let's get this consultation started, and if he shows up, he shows up."

I told the lawyer my story and he asked a bunch of questions and took a bunch of notes. At 2:30, he glanced at the clock, and said, "Looks like that boyfriend of yours is a no-show."

"Fiancé" I corrected the lawyer.

I looked down at my hands, which were folded in my lap. As I turned my engagement ring around my finger, I tried to recall how many times over the last few years our wedding date had been changed. The excuses that had seemed so reasonable at the time no longer mattered. My fiancé was nowhere in sight. He had never answered my yeses with any of his own. My yeses and my love remained unrequited. I slid the ring off my finger and tucked it into my blazer pocket.

"*Former* fiancé," I added.

The lawyer paused. His shoulders slumped a little and his gaze seemed to soften slightly. "You were engaged to a myth. You need to understand this man is a figment of your imagination as far as the FBI is concerned. Do you have any photos of him? Any way to prove his identity?"

"He never wanted to have his photo taken, so that may take some time," I admitted. "I can give you his name and birthdate... "

"OK. Let's start there. Is there anything else?"

My former fiancé was driving a vehicle that was registered in my name, so the lawyer encouraged me to report it stolen as a strategy for bringing him in for questioning sooner rather than later. I filed a stolen vehicle report before leaving the lawyer's office.

The Undeniable Yes

Several days later, my former fiancé showed up at my house. When I saw the vehicle coming up the driveway, I called 911, as my lawyer had advised.

Thanks to an open window, thin walls, or both, he heard me placing the 911 call and became angry.

"Did you just report me? How dare you!" he tried to beat the door down. "You bitch! I'm going to kill you!"

He threatened me multiple times. I kept the dispatcher on the line the whole time so she could hear. I prayed the door would hold up to his kicking and pounding.

Thankfully, the door held. And when the sirens became audible in the distance, he abandoned his threats and drove away.

Two sheriffs arrived in separate vehicles. I directed one toward the direction my former fiancé had headed. The other, a female deputy, stayed with me to ask some questions. I showed her the door that was on the verge of breaking down after all the kicking and beating.

"Thank you for getting here when you did. I don't think the door would have held much longer."

The sheriff's deputy pushed her sunglasses to the crown of her head and squinted at me in the afternoon light. I avoided her gaze and picked at the peeling paint on the porch railing.

She stepped to the side as if to avoid the glaring sun. I could tell it was an effort to make eye contact, so I shifted to block the sun and meet her gaze.

"Does he abuse you?" she asked, point blank.

"Abuse? No, I don't think so. I wouldn't call it abuse, but we do argue a lot." I wondered if she could see the bruise on my leg from where he had kicked me during an argument a month ago. I hadn't gone to the doctor for fear he would hit me again if he found out — assuming I told the doc how I got the bruise in the first place.

"What do you typically argue about?" she asked.

"The usual stuff I suppose. Dishes in the sink. Leaves in the yard. Feeding the dogs. Changing the cat's litter box — he never wants to do any of that, by the way. Stuff like that."

"Tell me about the arguments."

I paused.

"Well, two weeks ago, he went for a run and he took one of the dogs with him. It was already 100 degrees out that morning. I told him not to go, but he didn't listen. When they got home, the dog died of heat stroke right over there in the driveway."

I paused, took a breath, and went on. "We had a screaming match then, over that poor dead dog's body. It wasn't just an I-told-you-so scolding. He had the nerve to try and turn the whole situation back around on me. He insisted it was my fault—that I was the one who had killed the dog. It was insane. I figured maybe it was just how he was dealing with his grief or something. I don't believe he woke up that morning with the intention of killing the dog. But that's what happened. And it made me mad that he tried to make it my fault when I didn't have anything to do with it. Hell, I was the one who warned him not to take the dog running in 100-degree heat in the first place."

The deputy nodded, prompting me to continue.

"He always does that—blames me for stuff he's done. He did something wrong on the Internet and now he's running from it and blaming me. But our day-to-day arguments are pretty senseless, really. Doesn't everyone do that?"

The deputy sighed. "I'm sorry about the loss of your dog. I'm curious to know if he ever abused any of your other pets?"

"She was such a pretty puppy—a Rottweiler mix with blue eyes. Only a year old. Very smart. It's too bad... No, I wouldn't say he's abused the other animals... " My voice trailed off as I realized how hard he would hit the dogs if they peed in the house (which only occurred when he left them inside too long). On one occasion, one of the dogs limped for a week afterwards.

"Well, it's something to think about," she said, "because what they do to animals, they'll do to people."

She took a deep breath and said, "If he's stalking you, it's probably more serious than you think. Let me give you this card. There are some people here who can help."

She handed me the business card for a local women's shelter. She didn't release the card immediately — and made sure we had eye contact as we both grasped it. "Sometimes it's hard to recognize things for what they are when you're in them," she said in a tone that sounded more like a concerned family member than a sheriff's deputy.

Later that evening, I called the women's shelter, out of curiosity more than anything else. I didn't feel like a "battered woman" but I was curious about this abuse thing. Maybe the deputy was right. Maybe I wasn't seeing the situation clearly because I was in it. The old saying that you can't see the forest for the trees is true on multiple levels. Besides, I must have been missing something for my relationship to have gone so terribly wrong.

The helpful, reassuring voice on the other end of the line asked me a series of questions aimed at determining whether I had been abused or not. I answered yes to every question she asked. I let the concept sink in: I had been abused.

At that point, my fear began a slow turn toward anger. Anger at myself for not seeing it sooner. Anger for letting the relationship go on. Anger for letting it be a relationship at all. It was an anger born of clarity — the fog had begun lifting and I recognized myself as someone who had been subjected to abuse. I began to form some self-determination that I would heal myself and never let this happen again. I wanted to share my life with someone. To have a relationship.

A truly loving relationship... not like this. Whatever it took. What was it about me that had allowed this to happen, why hadn't I been able to see it for what it was in real time?

By admitting I had been abused, I could say yes to a different future for myself. From now on, I would say yes to healing and self-growth, and prevent this kind of thing from happening again in my life with anyone else.

The Unapologetic Yes

The day-to-day seriousness of the situation took a heavy toll on my physical and mental health. My back went out and my mind went numb, as if to protect itself from a constant state of fear and self-loathing.

Looking back now with nurse's training, I see that I was having an acute stress reaction. Yet, that's not what my doctors called it then. My healthcare providers were ready and willing to offer multiple pharmaceutical solutions, but they were prepared to offer little else. And it was precisely the "what else" that I needed. In short, the traditional Western medical system failed me in my quest for healing.

My doctor prescribed muscle relaxants, which I didn't react well to. They made me feel out of control, altered my mind in an unpleasant way — and literally took away my will to move and even live. I flushed the meds down the toilet and went to the chiropractor, which helped me get moving functionally so I could at least get through the day. The chiropractor referred me to a massage therapist, who introduced me to essential oils and Reiki, among other amazingly wonderful holistic tools for self-care. Fortunately, these tools got me walking upright in short order, and helped me stay functional.

It wasn't just my body that was in rebellion. My mind wasn't right in the aftermath either. I couldn't concentrate, I couldn't sleep, and I began having panic attacks. In a beneficent show of support for me and my future, my employer offered to pick up the tab for me to see a psychiatrist.

I had never seen a psychiatrist before, and I envisioned sessions "on the couch" to help me process the concept of abuse. I was eager to take a self-exploratory journey to help me understand what had happened, repair my mind, and prepare for future relationships. I felt confident that processing my emotions would help me heal the part of myself that had allowed this to happen so it would never happen again.

To my surprise, the psychiatrist did not seem interested at all in what had happened or what I wanted to explore. During my first session, she failed to ask any questions whatsoever about my symptoms or my feelings. She launched immediately into reciting a list of drugs, along with their benefits and side effects. Her recitation had a casual air, like a coworker listing off the takeout menu items from the local sandwich shop. She concluded with a query: Which one did I want? I was so surprised by this approach that I had no immediate response. She interpreted my silence as consent, and proceeded to recommend certain options.

In an out-of-body moment, I heard myself cutting off her recommendations with a half-shouted, "No!"

Notably, this statement was not a "no Ma'am," or a "no thank you." It was a full-throated, definitive verbal line-in-the-sand. A single staccato syllable born of certainty, clarity, and heartfelt authentic conviction. I didn't realize it then, but this statement was, in effect, an unapologetic yes to my true self, my whole health, and my fully empowered future.

She paused, and peered at me curiously over her half-glasses with one eyebrow raised, her mouth partially open.

"That won't be necessary," I continued in a softer, yet confident tone. "I don't need drugs right now; I need reassurances and protection. I'm facing the very real possibility of going to jail for something I didn't do. And I've just realized the man I agreed to spend the rest of my life with is a violent criminal, a con-artist, and a stalker. These are not things drugs can help me with. I'll seek help elsewhere."

Without waiting for her reply, I gathered up my notebook and purse. I stood tall, squared my shoulders, and walked out of her office with a confident stride. A renewed sense of clarity and strength flowed through me. I had no idea where "elsewhere" might be. I could not predict where the help I so obviously needed would come from, but I knew for certain it would not arrive in pharmaceutical form.

Yes, Mom. Yes, Dad. Yes, God.

Sometimes the best help you'll ever get is right in front of you all along. You simply need to pay attention. Fortunately, I was able to say yes to accepting the sage advice provided to me at the time by my mom, my dad, and ultimately, God. Doing so actually led to a spiritual awakening for which I am eternally grateful.

When I let my parents know what had happened, my mom responded with two memorable nuggets of advice: "First of all," she said, "he [meaning my former fiancé] doesn't get to win." And second, she admonished me, "Don't be angry at God."

It struck me as odd that my mom would see the situation as some sort of a competition, where my fiancé might "win" and I might "lose." And yet, that's precisely what it was. I learned through my lawyer that my former fiancé was a con-artist known to the law enforcement community. So my mom had a point. If I lived in fear or showed weakness in any way, he'd win. Which was an unacceptable outcome. There was a strong lesson of determination and setting a winning mindset here. An opportunity to stand up for myself, and not be a victim.

The other thing was that it never would have occurred to me to be angry at God. God hadn't really entered into the picture for me since I left home to go to college. And maybe that was part of the problem. Maybe I would benefit from checking in with God more often. So I started reciting Psalms 23 as a form of meditation whenever I took a daily walk. This practice made me feel more connected and confident. Interestingly, it paved the way for me to learn all sorts of mystical skills and techniques for connecting with the Divine in the years to come.

My dad likewise offered up his best advice: He told me that I must not live in fear, and that I would eventually get through the situation. "Fear is the mind-killer," he reminded me, quoting one of our favorite childhood books, *Dune*. He reminded me that I'd need to keep my wits about me in the weeks and months to come, and preserve my ability to think clearly to plan my next move as I navigated the situation. He also had a message of perseverance for me: Sometimes "the only way out [of a bad situation] is through [it]."

I was fortunate to have this good advice to galvanize me because my former fiancé proved to be a relentless stalker. In one memorable contact, I didn't recognize the number he was calling from so I answered his call.

He asked, with a breathless air of desperation, "I need to know one thing. Do you still love me?"

What was my truth here? I paused and took a deep breath before letting my soul speak. "Yes... in a Christian sense," was my heartfelt response.

He waited so long before answering that I thought the connection was lost. "You sound strong," he said. There was a hint of fear and an edge of defeat in his voice. Then he hung up.

In this moment I realized I truly loved myself. In spite of all of my mistakes and shortcomings. Because I loved myself, I could generously love my fellow human being, even if he'd done me wrong. I had said yes to my truth with an authentic voice.

Love your neighbor as yourself. The Golden Rule. I'd heard it a thousand times in Sunday School and church growing up. And I didn't realize until then that they leave out the most important part: You have to love yourself first, before you can ever hope to love anyone else... in a Christian sense, or any other way.

I realized I had never actually loved myself before. I was waiting for someone else to tell me he loved me and that would do the trick. I had misunderstood. The truth is, love comes from within. It springs eternal from the divine connection we all have inside us. So in that moment, I could honestly answer, yes, "I love you" in a Christian sense.

Saying yes to standing in my own power by declaring boundaries, intending victory and trusting that God would see me through the situation ultimately led to a significant spiritual awakening that continued to grow and blossom from this point forward. Ultimately, I became a better, more evolved human being because of all of this. Things were happening around me and to me, and this situation rattled me into taking ownership of the situation.

Claiming Yes

In the years since I said yes to a marriage proposal for all the wrong reasons, I've said yes to many other opportunities for all the right ones. I've responded positively to a cascade of significant yeses in my life. Each yes has contributed to my ability to love myself, access my own spirituality, stand in my own power, and speak with an authentic voice. Here's how claiming yes as a territory of inner discovery and exploration has helped me to lock in those key lessons:

- I said yes to learning to use firearms safely and develop my marksmanship skills. What I learned about myself from firearms training was I can create a safe environment for myself. I have the power to defend myself, my home, and my loved ones.
- I said yes to rescuing a mule that had also been abused. From this experience, I learned that I can take care of others. I can have adventures.
- I said yes to learning to work with biofield energy and harness it for healing. I learned to read Akashic Records and do Reiki, and much later, became certified in Healing Touch. My connection to the Divine is a tool that can be used to help others as well as myself, and I can teach others how to connect also. From these experiences I learned to trust my intuition and I began to see it as a tool that can be harnessed for healing.
- I said yes to working a full season as a camp cook and backcountry trail guide at a wilderness pack station. I can lead others on adventures and create a safe environment for them.
- I said yes to furthering my education by graduating from nursing school and being licensed and board certified as a Family Nurse Practitioner. I can care for others and share what I've learned about healing.

- I said yes to a right relationship and marriage. I can connect with another human being in relationship.
- I said yes to learning transformational coaching as a tool to help others help themselves.
- I said yes to becoming an entrepreneur to build a platform for sharing what I've learned with others. I am honoring a calling to help others help themselves.

The Divine Yes

That episode in my life informs me, yet it does not define me. The experience made me a better person. I am grateful for all that I learned. Before my experience of survival, I was naive, socially blind, and spiritually disconnected and could not have lived to my fullest potential.

I discovered that sometimes saying the right yes — the authentic yes, the yes that is true to the Self — actually means saying no.

My healing journey continues to this day, and my story's not yet complete. I spent ten years learning techniques of healing, ten years exploring nursing as a way of delivering what I've discovered. And now it's time to deliver my gifts.

The key is DOING the work. Every day I practice saying the right yeses. Every day I practice standing in my own power, accessing my spirituality, advocating for holistic healing, and speaking with an authentic voice. Every day I expand my experience of self.

Twenty years post-survival, I can honestly say I love myself more fully and completely than I ever could have otherwise. Surviving abuse helped me experience my true Self. My view of yes grew and expanded and changed everything for me. Yes is a three-letter word that holds more power and value than we can possibly imagine.

Lane Therrell inspires and empowers others to heal. In her health coaching practice, she integrates a wide variety of experiences as a board-certified Family Nurse Practitioner, educator, and energy healer. When she's not helping patients, clients, or students, she's enjoying the great outdoors.

DailyInspiredHealth.com

CHAPTER FIVE

Knowing Who You Truly Are

Rosie Battista

When you don't know who you truly are, the Universe will conspire to help you find out.

One day a few months short of my fiftieth birthday, I found myself on the basement floor on my hands and knees. I'd had enough. Under what seemed to be a torrential storm of black clouds teeming down buckets of crap into my life, I asked God to tell me what to do.

I had always chosen the hard way. I had always chosen to struggle.

Because I didn't know who I truly was, I always looked for things outside of myself to make me enough, and it caused unnecessary pain and suffering.

I looked for love in all the wrong places. Looking in the refrigerator got me an eating disorder and looking for a loving partner got me two divorces.

Because I didn't know who I truly was, I showed up dependent on others to love me. I thought that other people were the key to my happiness. I thought it was someone else's job to make me happy.

I tried to fill the void with something else. My addiction was food, manifesting in a binge eating disorder that I suffered with for thirty-plus years.

On my knees that day, I asked God for an answer.

I was recently divorced for the second time, my last child was going off to college, my eating disorder was in full swing while my business was in the toilet, and I was about to lose my home.

This was my dark night of the soul, which I would later learn is a good thing. Your soul wants you to drop away all that doesn't serve your highest good. This is clean-up time and the dark night leads you to the light.

I know now what surrender looks like. Because I had no idea what to do, and I was sick of trying to figure it out on my own, I literally handed it over.

And then what I heard was, "Enter a bodybuilding competition."

Two months shy of my fiftieth birthday and forty pounds overweight, this was a wild one. But I grabbed onto what felt like a rescue rope to pull me up from the darkness.

I responded with a yes.

It wasn't without trepidation because as my ego kicked in I started to think, *What the hell are you doing? It's too late for you to do this.* I started to question my Universal whisper.

For a figure competition, you have to achieve the perfect amount of muscle and tone, you have to exhibit grace and flexibility, you have to show balance and control, you have to show up in a very skimpy bling bikini, all while donning four-inch heels (and without tripping across the stage). And while not smearing any of the three layers of spray tan meant to show off the muscles, standing in front of an audience and judges, prancing and posing to your chosen song.

If that doesn't sound challenging enough, add in that there is no category for a fifty-year-old woman. A fifty-year-old woman gets lumped into the thirty-five-year-old "and up" category. I'll add that on my competition day, the next oldest woman after me was forty-two years old.

So there's that.

And then there are the people.

There are the people whose opinion you don't ask for but who will give it to you anyway. There are those who subtly suggest you're crazy to do something so extreme. There are those who flat-out roll their eyes. There are friends intent on saving your butt, who believe that talking you out of it is their grand attempt to rescue you from destruction. There were even those who, three-quarters of the way through the process, tried to convince me to just stop it.

When you don't know who you truly are, you attract the people who agree that you're not good enough. People showed up mirroring to me the doubts that were already floating around in my own head. This didn't help the situation, because at that point, I was wishy-washy with my decision. I had friends say, "Why are you so obsessed with your body?" and "Why do you have to be so extreme about things?" and "What are you trying to prove?"

It was my son who saved me from myself. I must've asked him for the fiftieth time what he thought about my entering the competition. Did he think I could do it? Did he think I was too old? And he finally said to me, "Mom please, if you want to do it, DO IT or STOP talking about it."

For whatever reason that little suggestion was like a big bang, and is the one that took root as finally firmly planting the decision. I went immediately to book a show sixteen weeks away and marked it in my calendar.

This kind of timing (sixteen weeks) is almost physically impossible to attain, which makes it even more amazing that I actually did it. There was no room for error. But at that time it never dawned on me to pick a date that was further out. My food coach/ trainer told me he didn't really think I was going to do it. Thank God he saved his confession for the day after the show.

This is why I believe there was divine intervention on that basement floor that day. I know that the reason I succeeded was because I believed I could. On the day of the show, I was the exact weight I was supposed to be. Exactly to the number. I know... crazy, not crazy. Divine intervention is not something to be messed with. I learned that first-hand.

Marking that sixteen-week deadline in writing and sealing it with the participation fee, is what I call burning all ships behind me, leaving me no way to turn back. All I needed to do were all the things it would take to get me ready to show up on my appointed competition date.

I knew I had to focus all of my attention on this journey. That included getting mentally and physically prepared. It meant counting every single morsel of food that I ate. It meant completing workouts, often twice a day, strength training and cardio. It meant getting the right balance between losing weight and gaining muscle. It meant weighing myself every morning and reporting the results to my food coach, who would adjust my meal plan accordingly. It meant preparing six meals a day. It meant getting enough rest. It meant no socializing or playing because I had to keep my focus and my strength. It was literally a full-time job and I had to adjust my business accordingly, with the competition taking complete priority.

I realize now that the preparation became a meditative sort of state. A ritualistic type of living and loving on myself. Spending every moment with me, myself and I — with zero distractions.

Looking back, I believe this is why I was handed this particular rope. It was a rope that got me to quiet down, slow down, stay laser focused and stay with myself long enough to get to know me a little deeper. It was a rope that had me defy all limiting beliefs I had placed upon myself and what was possible.

Details, Details

Next there were the body details. The waxing, uh-huh, *everywhere* — because when I say little teeny weeny bikini, I mean it. I'll leave that there.

Getting dressed for competition day actually starts weeks before. You have to custom order your suit based on the size you anticipate being, not the size you are. Try that one on for size. It ain't easy. My teeny, weeny competition suit was black with pink roses (not pink polka dots), adorned with Swarovski crystals and rhinestones so I'd bling from the stage as I strutted my stuff. The suit must be in good taste, not too revealing but revealing enough. And don't forget the body glue. You have to glue this thing onto your skin so that nothing unexpected pops out of the little strips of fabrics that hold you all together.

Then there's the tanning, which begins a few days beforehand because you need several coats to look as "real" as can be. The tanner you are, the more your muscles pop. This requires multiple coatings over a period of days. There are professional tanners whose job it is to make you look natural, not orange. And then you can't shower because it will wash off. So you must time it all perfectly and avoid getting wet or sweaty after the final perfect spray.

Of course, don't skimp on the hair, makeup, and nails. All of these things count in the overall appearance and judging because a full general assessment and healthy appearance are part of the grading process. Grace counts big-time because you need a small degree of muscularity, overall muscle tone, shapely lines, overall fitness but not too lean, and makeup and skin tone must be radiant, but not too theatrical. This perfect presentation is not easy.

Then there's the music to walk out to. You've got to get just the right song that fits your personality. You've got to vibe with the music because you're posing to it... which brings me to another point. You need a posing coach. You need to practice posing. And you need to practice posing while walking in those four-inch heels.

I chose the song, "Amazing Just the Way You Are" by Bruno Mars. To this day, I cry every time I hear that song, as it immediately pulls me right back to that moment.

That big walk onto the stage is your grand moment. All of the hard work and dedication comes down to this. They announced my name and then in front of an audience of strangers, family, friends, and a row of judges glaring at me, I did my thing.

The judges looked over every inch of me. After posing, I stood in a line. They moved me around to stand next to different competitors in order to compare my glutes, my abs, my thighs, my arms to my neighbors. They continued by moving the highest-ranking favorites to one side and the not-so-faves to the other side.

I kid you not.

You might be asking right now, Who in their right mind would want to subject themselves to all of this judging, comparing, picking apart?

I've thought about this many times since. When I pieced it together, I realized I'd spent much of my life doing exactly that to myself. Picking apart, judging, comparing not only my body but everything else about me too. I don't think there's a better example of an ironic situation.

The big shebang of this competition made it crystal clear.

It was when the individual eyeballs, the lights, and flashing cameras were all on me, that I stepped out of my body and floated above it. Rays of light shot down through the top of my head, causing shivers all over me. Thank God for the waxing so there was no hair on my arms to stand at attention. At that moment, all of me was at full attention. A totally surreal moment in time. And the moment that I woke up and I knew.

"Everything you need is inside of you."

That is not only what I heard, but felt all over my body. The Universe had set this up perfectly to send me the message in the perfect way for me — in the way that I could hear it. It was at this moment that my inner strength was revealed to me. It was at this moment that I knew I had to tell everyone about this wonderful message — that if it was inside of me, it was inside all of us.

A few days after the competition, I recognized the three powerful principles that got me through my sixteen-week journey and that would become what I share with others.

"Lose the fake stuff and get real" was the first principle that popped up for me.

At first glance it applied to the food I was eating. I really had to clean up and simplify my diet, which consisted of purely whole foods, lots of veggies, pro-tein, some fruit, and simple fats like avocado and nuts. Simple, clean, whole, and something I refer to as naked food (food in its most natural form, as God created it). But more importantly, "lose the fake stuff and get real" meant los-ing all the crap in my life that was fake and phony. All the fake and phony rules I made up about what I could do and could not do. All the phony friendships of people who did not allow me to be me.

The fake stuff was a compilation of limiting beliefs that I would base my life decisions on. Limiting beliefs were the reasons I said no to things I wanted, because I thought I couldn't have them or wasn't worthy of having them. They are what I lovingly refer to as B.S. (short not only for bull but for belief system). It's your belief system that is filled with limiting beliefs that need to go bye-bye. I began to replace those with ideas of what was really possible for me. The good news is that anything and everything is possible when you take away the limitations.

When you know who you truly are, you know that there is nothing standing in your way. My daily mantra became "I believe that miracles happen every day and that anything is possible." This first principle alone changed the way I was living my life. It opened doors I never even noticed were there. It gave me the opportunity to step through. I could have thrown in the towel at any point prior to the show. No one would have cared. I would have lost a few hundred dollars.

I didn't do that. Instead, I stepped through and went for it, which allowed me to discover all kinds of things about myself. It was like a doorway to me, to get to know more about myself.

When I decided I was done feeling not good enough, less than, or even too much, I let go of leading the show. In its place, I let God take over. That's when everything fell into place.

The second principle was "Become less interested in why you can't." This one involves the ego. The ego has very insidious ways of jumping in with a wreck-ing ball. It won't ever allow peace. Don't get too mad at it; that's its job. It loves when you pay attention to it, because that's what gives it power. It is fed by your attention. When you feel any emotions that are not love-based, you know your ego is involved. Its job is to wreak havoc.

For me, ego was insistent that I had wasted my life, made poor choices in love and money, and deserved to lose my house. It was insistent that I was too old to enter this competition, that my time for that had passed, and questioned why I thought I could get on that stage at that age.

It became evident to me that becoming less interested in why I can't was the key to having what I wanted. The ego loves trash-talking conversations and it loves to throw you off your game just when you think you've mastered it. The more I concentrated on trash talk and what I couldn't do, the more I felt defeated. That was my ego winning.

Every time, and there were plenty of them, that my ego popped in to take center stage whispering un-sweet nothings, I decided to say something different. I began to say, "Thanks for sharing but I'm not interested." And oh boy, this was perfect. It worked divinely, like a charm. The ego is starved when you ignore it. It loses power when you don't feed it with your fear. The truth is that if you believe you can't, you will be right. Therefore, the reverse is also true: if you think you can, you'll be right too.

And finally, the third principle that grew out of my figure competition was "Fall in love with the idea." This one is my favorite principle. Falling in love with the idea meant switching my attitude to "I get to" rather than "I have to." There was a point about halfway into my competition journey when I was really tired. Exhausted, cranky, hungry, with sprinkles of defeat spreading in my head and body, I began to question what I was doing and whether I should keep going.

In the middle of my waver, I had a God-wink. I remember exactly where I was standing and what I was feeling at the time it happened. It was one of those instances that changes your direction. Right at this crossroad, came the message: *Fall in love with the figure competition right now. You GET to do this Rosie, you don't have to.*

Having had the pleasurable experience of falling in love, I knew first-hand that when you do, all bets are off. You focus on that love and nothing else seems to matter. Love makes this so much more palatable. And the fact that I would get to do it, and was not forced to, gave me the freedom to make the choice. I could make this hard or I could make this fun. The choice was mine. So I chose wisely.

The magic of this moment looked like me falling in love. It looked like me getting excited that I had the health and the wherewithal to enter a figure competition. I began to feel grateful instead of cranky. This is the principle I used to complete my journey to the stage. When you stay in a state of love, God works through you and your life mirrors the states of God, which are love, peace, joy and happiness.

These three principles became my pattern interrupt, which shifted my life for the better. They gave me the opportunity to focus on something different and take a different direction than I might have chosen before. These principles continue to apply to any area of my life that feels stuck or that I want to improve.

When you know who you truly are, everything changes.

I know now what I blocked from my view back then. I know now that I am as God created me and that there are no limits unless I place them on myself.

Everything you need comes from within. When you live from within, your life on the outside mirrors that. The more love you have for yourself, the more it appears in your outside world. You live from the love inside you. You no longer look for love to fill you from the "any one" or the "any thing." You know that it's been inside and available to you the whole time. You know. You just know.

When you remember who you truly are, you make different loving choices for yourself and others. Better relationships show up, magical opportunities, and boat loads of abundance.

Every one of us is on the path to knowing. Every one of us has our one unique way of getting there. Sometimes I wish I had known sooner that I am a Spark of the Divine, a Goddess, and perfect as God created me. I could have avoided a lot of painful choices made to the contrary. Then I remember that I can't go back and fix the past, but I can stay right here and now, in the only time that matters, and enjoy the benefits of my ah-ha's that were gifted to me that day on that stage.

Please don't ask if I won a trophy. I did not. What I won doesn't need dusting or shelf space. What I won was my freedom. The freedom of knowing who I am changes everything, every decision, every choice, every opportunity that shows up for me.

Although it took a physical challenge and body transformation to wake me up, the shift is never external. It's in your heart and soul the whole time.

Rosie believes that miracles happen every day and anything is possible. She teaches clients to let go of limiting beliefs, allowing them to freely tap into their innate inner gifts.

RosieBattista.com

CHAPTER SIX

Second Chance

Michelle Garrett

I woke up disoriented, angry, and disappointed. Once again, I had failed at something that I had put so much time and effort into. I had planned out the details for almost a year, and while I thought I had a solid plan, I failed at yet another thing. That seemed to be the story of much of my adult life.

I could barely remember the previous twenty-four hours, but quickly realized that at some point my family had intervened.

I didn't move as the door opened.

"Michelle, if I was to let you go home, would you try to hurt yourself again?"

I had no response. I felt nothing. The thought of existing made everything within me ache. I had made my peace with suicide. There was no Plan B. All of these thoughts were racing through my mind, but the words could not find a way to leave my mouth.

Because I didn't have an answer, a choice was made for me. I spent the next week involuntarily committed to the psychiatric ward at a local hospital.

I learned more about myself during that time than I would have ever imagined. There were people committed right alongside me who I probably never would have connected with in my daily routine, but we were thrust together to heal. Many of us had a similar story. Somewhere along our journey, we had stopped making ourselves a priority and had ignored the pleas for help that our minds and bodies were sending out.

For years, I ignored the unsettling feeling that something was "off" in my life.

My focus and attention were on my family, business, community, friends — everything but me. I often felt like a fraud while speaking to women about the importance of loving themselves, putting their needs first, and creating a routine that included self-care.

I had made all of those things a priority in the past. Each of those things were vital to thriving personally and professionally. I knew all of that and tried my hardest to practice what I preached. But as I slipped deeper into depression, they fell lower and lower on my list of priorities. At some point, my life became robotic. I performed the roles that I knew I needed to fulfill, but felt completely removed and detached from everything.

The deeper my depression, the more my body just shut down. I was always exhausted. I would wake up each morning planning my nap for the afternoon. I stopped getting up with my children each morning to see them off to school. No matter how hard I tried, I couldn't do the "normal" things a wife and mom should do. I would take weekend getaways to my hometown and instead of spending precious family time or reconnecting with friends, I would enjoy glorious sleep in the house I grew up in. My Daddy would inquire about how I was feeling and it was difficult to put the words together to explain. My default answer became, "I'm just tired."

I'm often asked why I didn't just speak up and ask for help. It sounds so easy and simple to do, but when you're down, the words "I need help" come across in different ways to different people. I recall visiting my doctor frequently to see what I needed to do just to feel somewhat functional in my daily life. I wanted enough energy to engage with my family again and not continuously retreat to the comfort of my bed or favorite cozy spot on our couch.

I went to therapy. I poured out so much of what I had been holding in for years to a complete stranger. During our time together, I touched on so many events over the years that I had pushed far down. I would leave those sessions feeling raw and wide open. We discussed medication, and I was assured by multiple therapists at the office that that was not something I needed.

One afternoon I mentioned problems in my marriage. From there everything quickly went downhill. The following sessions involved the therapist attempting to convince me to leave my husband and rebuild my life on my own. As much as I tried to explain that that was not the core issue or even something I was ready to touch on, she dug her heels in deeper. I stopped going and my feelings of despair got worse.

I saw numerous medical doctors. I went through a battery of tests to determine the cause of my extreme fatigue, weight gain, and migraines. I did sleep studies, went on special diets, discovered I had a Vitamin D deficiency, began taking medication for migraines, and tried so hard to just show up for those around me. I would go through moments of feeling better and then quickly crash.

After four months of trying different things, my doctor finally told me his diagnosis: I was extremely obese and needed to lose weight. Simple as that. Lose the weight and I would get better sleep, be more energized, and find my joy again.

Those words left me completely defeated. I had been self-conscious about my weight for some time and no matter how much I tried, I could not get the numbers on the scale to go down. It seemed like the more I tried, the more I gained. So I stopped trying. Everything.

I no longer had the energy or desire to do anything. I notified my clients that I was taking some time away. Friends and loved ones were slowly put at a distance. I found comfort in my good friend Sleep. During that time I did not have to worry about how I felt or who I was letting down.

As I drifted off to sleep one day, an idea took form and grew roots. In my current state, I was constantly letting down my husband and children because I just did not feel motivated to do anything.

Depression truly gives a false sense of reality to your circumstances. The problem is, you can't see the true view until you're out of your depressive state. No matter what others say or do, your mind believes what it believes. Over time, I drew what seemed like rational conclusions based on my mindset.

I found a way to trace back every negative thing in my life, my family's life, and my business to me and my ineptitude. After a while, the logical conclusion was to remove myself from the equation.

When you hit rock bottom, there's hope and possibility in the escape. Often, you feel as though you have exhausted all options and choices. Yes, I reached out to multiple loved ones. I had gotten so used to not prioritizing and valuing my feelings and emotions that I could not adequately express the agony I was experiencing. I was the strong one. That person who everyone depended on. How could I be facing something I did not know how to manage?

I had thought through the ramifications of my actions. A detailed plan was in place to ensure my family's life continued seamlessly. Of course, now that I am in a place of healing, I realize how flawed my thinking was. There are moments when the thought of the pain I caused them, hurts more than the years of depression I endured.

My time in the hospital was like a giant buzzer and pause button being pressed at the same time. I had no choice but to focus on me. Doctors, therapists, and group leaders pushed me to answer the difficult questions and face years of repressed feelings and experiences. My release was dependent upon a judge who knew nothing about me deciding whether and when I was ready to go home. On visiting days, my husband came and sat. We were able to open up in ways we never had before, and it changed the course of our marriage.

I was terrified to call my mother. I knew the moment I heard her voice I would completely break down because I had, yet again, caused her pain and frustration. Since my teenage years, I had felt like I was a constant disappointment to her. I wanted so badly to be the daughter she had prayed for and envisioned raising. But I seemed to continuously fall short.

The love that I heard in her voice left me speechless. As I shared with her the visiting information and days, she matter-of-factly said she had already made plans to be on the road the next day. There was no judgment or questions. During her visit, she said all she wanted was for me to do what I needed to do for myself and that she was there for me no matter what. I didn't realize how much I had been yearning to hear those words from her throughout my life. Don't get me wrong, I always knew I was loved and wanted. The walls I had built over the years had blocked my view of just how much those I loved the most were there for me. At that moment, those walls started to come down.

One morning I had a conversation with one of the older ladies who was there. I can still remember the sound of her cries the first night she arrived. She was confused and scared. I stayed up most of the night praying for her until she calmed down. After a few days, she settled in and we had gotten into a routine of having a quick Bible Study together before breakfast. She looked at me and started speaking about the things she saw in me. She shared that she could tell how giving and nurturing I was and that I embodied the traits of the Proverbs 31 Woman.

"Oh, no ma'am! I'm far from her. I don't think I'll ever measure up to be the woman that's being described in that Scripture."

She immediately stopped me and began speaking words of strength, peace, and overall joy into my life. Many of the things she said aligned directly with prayers I had prayed, words I had written in my journals over the years, and desires of my heart that I had not shared with anyone.

That experience opened my eyes and heart. In that moment, in that space, I began my journey to healing. I realized there was truly a reason I was still here. The circumstances around my family getting me to the emergency room when they did was nothing but divine intervention. Hundreds of miles away, my mother could tell something was wrong and pushed for loved ones to physically put their eyes on me. If she hadn't, I most likely wouldn't be here.

"This moment doesn't define you. You're not the first person who has been at this point, and you won't be the last. What matters most is what you do next. You've been given the opportunity to begin again. Never take that for granted."

I can still hear my favorite nurse saying those words to me before I was discharged. Feelings of fear, apprehension, and overwhelm were setting in. I knew I needed to begin the process of living in the real world again, but there was comfort in being protected and sealed off from the rest of the world. What if I couldn't take the pressure? What if I wasn't good enough? The list of questions was endless.

At some point, I realized the blessing of hitting rock bottom is that there is plenty of room for improvement. As I worked to put the pieces back together, I completely walked away from my business. Considering I had been stagnant for more than a year, it was not that difficult to do. I disconnected from everything. For months, my days consisted of outpatient therapy, cuddle time with my daughter, long phone calls with my Daddy, family game nights, early morning breakfasts with my oldest son, and ending my day just talking with my husband before falling asleep.

Throughout my healing journey, I was blessed to cross paths with people from all walks of life who understood and walked similar paths. There was no judgment. Only love, acceptance, and encouragement to continue working on myself. Am I in a happier place? That answer changes from day to day. There is no magic cure for depression — especially depression that has gone untreated for such a long time. I once got frustrated with how long it was taking me to feel "normal" and was asked how long it took me to get to my lowest point. There were years and years of experiences that got me there. So expecting to be "cured" in a fraction of that time was unrealistic. I did not like that answer in the moment, but it made total sense.

As I continue to heal, I am learning to do the work I am called to do in a way that benefits my clients and community, but within the capacity I can handle. I speak more about mental wellness with the women I work with who are building businesses and brands. When I begin to feel stressed or stretched, I step away. That moment of disconnect means I am honoring what I need over what others need from me. Not everyone always understands that.

The biggest lesson I have learned and strive to pass to others is how important it is to make ourselves a priority. It's trendy to say those words. But it could be a matter of life or death if we consistently choose not to do so. It may not be depression or anxiety, but it could be health issues we ignore. It could be sleep that we neglect. Family members and memories we miss out on.

Yes, our businesses are important to us. For many, it's our true passion and purpose to do what we do. However, if we ignore our basic needs — what good are we to anyone? All of the dreams and big ideas we have to make a difference and help others, mean nothing if we are not here to see them through. The money we're earning to purchase that new home or take that family vacation is useless if our family does not have us fully present to enjoy those moments.

Stepping away momentarily to care for yourself is worth it if it means that you are healthy and whole to show up for those you care for the most. I learned that lesson the hard way, but I'm thankful for the second chance to do better and be a better version of myself.

Michelle D. Garrett lives in Columbia, South Carolina, with her husband and their youngest two children. In her work as a business and accountability coach for female entrepreneurs, Michelle teaches her clients the importance of setting actionable goals and making time for self-care, rest, personal growth, and time with loved ones a priority.

DivasWithAPurpose.com

The National Suicide Prevention Lifeline provides free and confidential support for people in distress, prevention and crisis resources for you or your loved ones, and best practices for professionals. Their lines are always open and available. If you feel more comfortable texting, the Crisis Text Line is a global not-for-profit organization providing free mental health texting services. From the U.S., you can text HELLO to 741741 and be connected with a Crisis Counselor.

CHAPTER SEVEN

Learning To Let My Light Shine

Benecia Ponder

The last time I drove a car, I was twenty years old.

It was a beautiful Monday morning and the normally congested Atlanta highway was miraculously traffic-free as I headed to work. Right before I was to get off at the exit that would lead to my office, a sharp pain hit me. Fighting a headache so fierce I could barely sit up, I don't know how I made it. I pulled into the parking lot and I couldn't get out of the car. My head throbbed, my body ached, and all I wanted to do was lie down. I sat in the driver's seat almost paralyzed; I was unable to move because of the pain. I finally mustered enough energy to crawl into the cramped backseat of my Ford Escort and lay there for four hours, until a co-worker could drive me home.

That was mid-January of 1999. Six months earlier, I'd finished my sophomore year at Emory University and had given birth to a beautiful baby girl. Determined not to let anything stop me from my desired success, I worked full-time during the day and pursued my undergraduate degree with a full course load at night. I had just been promoted at work, even though I was the youngest employee there, with the least amount of experience. I was also on track to finish my undergraduate degree on time with honors.

Suddenly all of that was on hold.

For the next three months I wound up in doctors' offices every day. They drew blood, did CAT scans and MRIs, and tried different steroids. My tests all came back normal, but the headaches kept happening. I had non-stop migraines; I couldn't eat and couldn't sleep.

None of the doctors could tell me what was going on — specialist after specialist, one probing and intrusive test after another. Three months of non-stop, agonizing pain continued with no answers.

Then one day something started going on with my eyes.

The doctor performed the test where you follow her finger with your eyes and I did fine, but I was back again the next day telling her something still wasn't right. She referred me to an ophthalmologist who saw me the same day (we had a great insurance plan). They handed me a book and to this day I have no idea what it was about, but I know I failed the test. Something was totally wrong. It's nearly impossible to describe — I could see clearly and yet I couldn't. It was there but it wasn't. My depth perception was off.

They sent me to a neuro-ophthalmologist who immediately said she knew what was going on and set up a spinal tap procedure.

I'm told that spinal fluid is supposed to flow... but mine squirted out and hit the technician. My spinal fluid pressure was about ten times what it should be and had been the source of my migraines.

I had pseudotumor cerebri, a condition in which the high pressure of the cerebrospinal fluid in the skull mimics the symptoms of a brain tumor.

One ten-minute procedure later, the pain was instantly gone, never to return again. I was ecstatic. I leaped for joy and praised God! I was healed!

My rejoicing didn't last long.

The prolonged buildup of spinal fluid pressure had irreparably damaged my optic nerves. I underwent a couple of surgeries on the optic nerve, but nothing helped. I was visually impaired and my whole world was fuzzy.

"If only you'd come in sooner," the neuro-ophthalmologist told me.

The diagnosis was March of 1999 and my daughter turned one in June of that year. From the time she was less than a year old, I haven't been able to clearly see her face or anything else more than a few inches in front of my face.

For months after my diagnosis, I flip-flopped between anger and depression. I can remember one day in particular when I was throwing a simultaneous pity party and temper tantrum on my bedroom floor: crying and begging, then pouting and demanding. I wanted to know what was going on. Didn't God know I had a baby who depended on me to take care of her? Didn't He know I had dreams of being something great? I remember asking God: "Why? What did I ever do that was so wrong?"

It was in the midst of this wailing and gnashing of teeth that I received a wake-up call. As clearly as if He was right in the room with me, I heard God telling me that my life was not over. A deep knowing stirred inside of me and I knew it was time for me to stop all the whining and complaining. It was time to stop using my present condition as an excuse to be less than my best.

My tears dried up and I determined from that day that I would not let my impaired vision prevent me from accomplishing whatever I wanted to accomplish.

No Time To Wallow

My family gave me a lot of support and encouragement. But they didn't treat me as if I was disabled in any way. They expected me to keep doing what I was doing.

It took me a couple of months to get to a place of "This is what it is." And I got busy learning how to navigate the world in a whole new way. I started taking classes at the Center for the Visually Impaired and learned mobility and life skills.

I applied to Georgia State University to finish my undergraduate work, starting up again in the fall of 2000, the year I was supposed to graduate from college.

I still wanted to finish school, so for the next two and a half years, I double majored in Management and Marketing, with a minor in Entrepreneurship. I was named the Business Student of the Year and won scholarships and awards in several Business School departments. I was determined to show everyone I was capable and could do anything I set my mind to do.

That's not to say I didn't still throw my pity parties from time to time. I remember watching my godsister, who graduated high school a year after me, graduate from college in 2001. I remember going to her graduation in Tallahassee, Florida, and then crying the whole way home. I was happy for her, but at the same time — why not me? I was really sad about that. There were times when I felt like things should have been different, but I didn't dwell on them. I kept moving, kept doing things, and hung out around people who expected me to just do — they didn't put qualifiers on it.

When I started school again, I took a full course load every semester. The Disability Services office at Georgia State helped with accommodations for testing, though most of the time, I didn't use it.

In fact, I usually wouldn't tell people I had a visual impairment. I had the option of taking tests in the Disability Services office where they could be enlarged, but I'd just do it in class instead. I didn't want people to think I was less than or to think something was wrong with me.

After graduating in the spring of 2003, I applied to law school. My sister, who is three years younger than me, had graduated high school, finished undergrad in three years, and was starting her second year of law school. I was in awe of her success and admired her tremendously. My own accomplishments seemed pale in comparison to my sister's stellar achievements, and I felt the need to show that I could do it too.

I applied to Georgia State College of Law and was admitted on the waitlist. With a tenacity fueled by my fear of failure, I hounded the admissions team, talked to professors, and showed them all the reasons they should let me in — and they did.

My fear of being perceived as weak or less than often led me to take action. Trying to prove that I was just as good as everyone else challenged me to excel.

The fear of failure never stopped me... but the fear of success certainly has.

In retrospect, I recognize times when insecurities about my visual impairment came into play. During my first year of law school, I excelled at debates and advanced to the highest levels in mock trial competitions. When an internship opportunity came up, I did great in the first round of interviews, and was told I was amazing and would get it.

The process included three steps. I did fine during the second step, a networking cocktail hour where we met people from big law firms and companies. But when it came time for the third step, the interview with an actual hiring panel, I froze.

The same thing had happened my last year of undergraduate school. I had applied for a job with a marketing company and during the interview, was asked a situational type of question. I knew the answer... yet said I didn't know what I would do.

Both times, I was so afraid of actually getting the position and not being able to do it without letting people know about my visual impairment that I sabotaged myself.

I don't think I've done that very often, though I still don't like to let on about my impairment. Most people don't know. I attend conferences in hotels I've never been to and I find my way around. If something is close enough, I can see it. If I can't, I'll ask how to get somewhere; when I get to the next spot, I can ask someone else for the next set of directions.

I did have a cane once, but I would only use it in the airport to get through security. My mobility instructor told me I need to use it to let people know I can't see, but that was the issue: I didn't *want* people to know. He convinced me to use it and one day, I was riding the bus home and overheard a couple of guys my age.

"She's too fine to be blind," one of them said... which was the worst thing I could have heard. People were judging me. I stopped using the cane.

I admit it: it's an ego thing where I don't want to appear vulnerable. Sometimes I wonder why I can't just tell people. And why can't I be great and let them know all parts of me? Is it affecting how I show up in the world, and am I passing on opportunities because I don't want people to judge me?

Today

I've accomplished a lot of things over the past twenty years of being visually impaired: I finished law school and passed the Georgia bar exam the first time; I started a consulting practice writing grants and business plans, and developing strategies that helped my clients generate more than $20 million; I was certified as a personal and executive coach and worked with clients all over the world; I have spoken on many stages; and I am the best-selling author of six books.

As much as I have accomplished, however, I have to admit that one of my greatest regrets is that I hid my visual impairment for so long. By hiding such a big part of me, not only did I give myself the subconscious belief that no matter how much I achieved I would always be less than, I also believe I missed out on a lot of opportunities to help others who might have been experiencing the same.

That's why I have been so dedicated over the past few years to helping others share their messages with the world. I founded ILLUMINATION Press, a publishing services company that helps inspired individuals write and publish amazing books. I love helping people take their expertise, that genius inside of themselves, and use it to help others. I'm even considering doing a collaborative book series by people who are more than abled, people who have what others call disabilities yet are doing amazing things.

Even without a physical or mental impairment, there are so many people in the world today who are disabled. I hope this brief glimpse into my journey has been a source of inspiration — a beacon of light to show others that they can accomplish great things, despite the challenges they might face.

The most difficult part of my journey wasn't the part where I lost my eyesight. It was when I feared what others might think and I lost my vision. It took me a long time to learn the lesson, but hopefully my story inspires others to figure it out sooner. Let your light shine!

Benecia Ponder is a multiple bestselling author, inspirational speaker, and award-winning entrepreneur. As founder of ILLUMINATION Press, Benecia is dedicated to helping individuals use their experiences and expertise to illuminate the world with books that make a big difference and a big profit.

InspirationalAuthors.com

CHAPTER EIGHT

The Spotlight
Maruxa Murphy

I was in a Walmart checkout line when my world as I knew it turned upside down.

It was October 2008 and I was twenty-eight years old. My oldest daughter Maya was just four weeks old and I decided to take her shopping with me at the local Walmart to pick up a few things to get us through the week.

I had in my hands my WIC check along with the beans, cheese, formula, milk, diapers, and a few other things that I knew I could cover with this government check.

Never in my life would I have thought I'd be in this situation. If you had met me just one year prior, you'd have met a highly ambitious woman making all of her professional dreams happen.

I was working in higher education as the youngest Director of Multicultural Affairs that Rollins College had ever hired. I was a part of leading a curriculum reform endeavor that would integrate leadership, identity development, and service into every college classroom experience, and I was teaching classes at the college on Intercultural Communication and Social Justice Through Film. I was innovating strategies for students, faculty, and staff to create and cultivate a new way of leading in the world... and I did all of this while finishing up my Master's degree in Mental Health Counseling. It was intense yet fulfilling. We were solving big problems and leading leaders, and I loved every minute of it.

Then September 2007 happened. My husband Dennis, who worked in the mortgage industry, came home two weeks after turning thirty to tell me that when he went to the office that day, he walked towards a building with chains and a padlock on the doors and a note that said:

"We are sorry to inform you that Option One Mortgage has closed. Please feel free to apply for Unemployment Benefits. Thank you."

He came home determined to find another opportunity. I wasn't worried. We had my $42,000-a-year salary. Living on one salary, we were able to manage living paycheck to paycheck without putting any money into our rainy-day fund. I had worried for a bit, but let it go because I was certain that within just a few weeks, my husband, one of the hardest-working men I know, would find another opportunity.

But that was not in the cards for us.

What we didn't know was that, in addition to his company, essentially the entire real estate industry would fall apart as well. When Dennis was let go, so were millions of others in the real estate and mortgage industries. Homes were being foreclosed on left and right, and even after sending out four hundred customized resumes, Dennis didn't get a single call back for an interview. It was depressing. He was taking minimum wage temp jobs to support us, doing everything and anything, from marketing to processing records to working at a pest control company, while applying for mid-level salaried positions.

However, because the word "mortgage" was on his resume, no one would touch him. Our friends in human resource careers told us that he wasn't even being looked at because he had the word "mortgage" on his resume. Companies were scanning all resumes that had the words "mortgage" or "real estate" out of the massive pool of leads, even though many like him had perfect qualifications for the positions they applied for.

In that same season of our lives, we found ourselves pregnant (surprise!) with our daughter Maya. This was a big deal because for six months before Dennis lost his job, we were trying to no avail to get pregnant. Here we were, filled with a mix of joy and anxiety about what life would be like for this sweet child. I was still insistent that he would find work, so no. big. deal. But again, I had no clue that that was not in our plans for quite some time.

I saw my husband struggle to stay positive as our now one salary was holding us steady without any cushion.

The problem was that while I was the one with the salary, I was also finishing up my 20-hour-per-week internship to obtain my Master's degree, pregnant, working 50-60 hours in my full-time job, and I was watching Dennis slip away into a deeper and deeper depression. Everything in me wanted to change this story for him, for me, and for this baby we were about to bring into this world. I couldn't see how we would be able to break out of this season.

So I kept adding on to my plate.

I decided this would be the PERFECT time to try to build a business! I created a relationship with a direct sales company to use my unique strategy as a leadership and identity development influencer with a Master's degree in counseling and see whether I could take these products I was selling and turn them into cash flow for our family.

Within three months of joining the company, I had a three-month waiting list for these spa experiences I was creating for women. I was bringing in cash to help pay the bills. Dennis was helping me sell the husbands and boyfriends at the back of the room, and we found a new way to cover our bills with this side business. The trouble was that as the pregnancy was progressing, my body couldn't keep up with the experience I built for these women, which often consisted of hauling tubs of water for each woman to soak her feet while I lead them through a visualization exercise and relaxation techniques.

The other problem was that the career I loved at the college needed more of me than I was willing to give once I became a mom. In fact, when I shared that I was pregnant, a well-meaning team member asked me when I was due. When I mentioned I was due mid-September, she crinkled her nose and reminded me that this was a very busy time of year to have a baby and asked when I would be able to get back into the office. In that moment, I knew I was growing beyond my capacity for this work and that I needed to figure out how to use my gifts, experiences, and talents in another way.

I also knew leaving my career in higher education because of having a child meant that I was choosing career suicide. I wouldn't be able to jump back in so naturally, and I recognized that this was a major decision I needed to make to be more aligned with what I wanted to create for myself and this family we were making.

I knew that Dennis hadn't found work yet, but at the same time, I knew I needed to shift my career to serve my needs and my family in the best way I could. It would be a long journey to get there, but I needed to stay true to what was coming up for me at that time.

Of course, being the eternal optimist that I am, I trusted everything would be ok. While Dennis took temp jobs and sent out resumes, I focused on that direct sales job to grow my sales and team. I was actually growing the team, and money was coming in! I was so proud of myself.

But the truth of the matter was: I didn't consider a lot of things.

For example, if you make 30 percent profit on each product, you think, "Great! I just made $300 from the $1,000 I just sold!"

What I didn't realize is that to stay and grow in the ranks, you need to spend a certain amount of money to continue elevating yourself in the direct sales journey. So if you made $1,000 in sales and wanted to continue with the awards and recognition for reaching whatever level (or goodness, you want to rise beyond that level!) you needed to buy more product to sell, and then continue to raise your status.

What I didn't know at that time was how that $300 that we desperately needed to help with bills would need to go toward MORE product in order to sell more and make more. The truth was that this path was so much slower than if I were to take on a low-paying job with a company.

I knew, however, that I was sparked by making my own money. I knew that what I was doing wasn't the path for me, but something within me lit up at the idea of creating money without having to work in a company, and I wanted to figure out how to create income on demand without feeling like I had to work myself to the bone to make it happen.

And yet, desire doesn't always mean reality.

Back To Reality

When I was in that Walmart in October 2008 with my four-week old Maya, I was just a few weeks removed from visiting the government assistance building in my town to apply for WIC (Women, Infants and Children) assistance. I started getting checks every two weeks to buy the basics to feed myself and my daughter. Bread, cheese, milk, beans, rice. Diapers and formula for her, if she needed it.

I felt defeated.

It was as if all the joy I had just one year prior was stripped from me. I couldn't see straight, and this depression that Dennis was climbing out of because of temp jobs was about to suck me under this time.

But I kept persevering. I needed to stay strong for more than myself now. I needed to stay strong for Maya, even if my ego was taking a massive hit.

So that day, I chose to use the WIC check I just received and challenge myself to take my just-fed-one-hour ago baby to Walmart with me.

As a brand new mom of a four-week old, I had no idea what would happen with a newborn who had just eaten one hour prior. Maya had had jaundice for a full week and I had left the hospital with Bell's Palsy, half my face paralyzed for a full eighteen days, from the stress of birth. I was desperate to get out of the house. I had no idea what I could/would do if she got hungry while I took my time slowly perusing the aisles, wishing I could buy more than what was allowed with this check.

But I soon found out.

At the end of my Walmart aisle travels, I knew it was about time to feed her but I kept putting that thought out of my mind because I had to buy the food. We got in the checkout line and she started screaming. I was trying hard to figure out what to do.

There was a line forming behind me, about four or five people deep. I could see them getting uncomfortable with her screaming. I was anxious about her screaming. I wanted to put my food on the conveyor belt, give the cashier the WIC check, and get out of there.

However, the cashier didn't appreciate that I didn't have two forms of ID.

In a very slow and deliberate voice, she spoke to me as if I didn't speak English. With eyes wide and holding up two fingers, she started to speak to me: "Do... you... have... two... forms... of... ID?"

I looked at her frazzled because while Maya was screaming and the line behind me was getting longer, I realized I forgot my second form of ID at home.

I told her that this was my first time out with my new baby and I was trying to figure this out with my daughter being only four weeks old, and I accidentally forgot my second form of identification. I spoke perfect English with the American accent I perfected when I was five years old, having just moved to the United States from the Philippines.

She rolled her eyes at me and again spoke to me as if I didn't speak English: "I'm... so... sorry... that... you... forgot... your... ID,... but... you... cannot... buy... this... food... at... this... time."

By then, Maya was completely hysterical. I was trying to console her. In the line right behind me was this beautiful older woman who I to this day call my Angel. She looked over at me and asked, "Honey, do you need me to pay for your food today?"

I looked at her in my complete and utter embarrassment at being treated as a second-rate person by the cashier while at least five other people witnessed this moment in my life. It was as if a spotlight was on me as I stood in that checkout line. I was absolutely stunned that we were in this position, with all of these accolades and with all of these awards under my belt, feeling like I'm a beggar, not able to feed my family.

I was so embarrassed that I ran away from the situation. I did what any other amazing woman would do, and left all my food at the cashier's counter and ran with my daughter into my car to cry my eyes out. I was a mess. I remember that minute so very clearly because for me it was a minute in my life where things were happening in slow motion. While I consoled and nursed my daughter, I sat there sobbing. I told myself this will never happen again. This moment in my life will never happen again.

I had no idea how we would get out of this situation, but I knew in that exact moment that my purpose was to overcome this Story I was playing into, that said we were always going to be dependent on others for jobs, for financial support, for direction. And I would share with other women how to build a life and a lifestyle that invited all of us to live from our higher selves instead of feeling like a victim to patronizing and power-hungry people and institutions. I wanted to learn how to create our own economy so that one day, I could invite other women into their own life's journey to create their own economy once and for all.

In the midst of the "spotlight" moment I had in Walmart, I called my husband, and in between my sobs I said to him, "Believe me. Hear me out. We are going to change this once and for all. We will never, ever feel like we are alone. We will never feel like we have to beg for food. We're going to teach our children to live a life that's so much more financially stable so that they can create a life they want to live. There will never be another time in my life where I will feel like I need somebody else to make my dreams happen."

Setting An Intention

While we were feeling completely helpless... we had added this feeling of shame.

Shame that we couldn't figure out how to do it all.

Shame that we were using credit cards.

Shame that we had to ask for help.

Shame that we were sitting in the dark, cold offices asking the government for money and food stamps.

Shame. Shame. Shame.

I get it. Food stamps and WIC checks are made for times like these. I, however, grew up with the idea that I can do anything. I was under the impression that government help meant I was lazy. I was not giving my all.

This was everything BUT our truth.

We were giving our all and I have never worked harder to get so little in return.

As a first-generation immigrant coming from the war-torn country of the Philippines, I moved into this ideology of the "American Dream." I would never expect to get government aid because I was supposed to use my gifts and talents to work and make the world a better place. How was I making this world a better place if I was getting help from the government?!

I just couldn't see it.

As a child, we lived a life of feast or famine. My parents did their best, but as first-generation immigrants, we were told that to "make it" in the United States, you have to work hard. My parents are some of the hardest workers I know. My mom would sometimes work 120 hours a week just to make sure her work was top quality, but that meant I often was put to bed by my aunts and other family members.

As the oldest, I was the one in charge of my siblings a lot as well. However, the bottom line was that the best thing we could do was get good grades, graduate, and get a good job with benefits. We weren't ever taught how to be the business OWNER. We weren't taught that some business owners and entrepreneurs were able to bless others with their gifts and vision. It wasn't until soon after this time in my life that I saw and worked with entrepreneurs who wanted to build businesses from a place of abundance and possibility.

I was that kid in the family who was always eager to build the next thing: a bake sale! A talent show! A babysitters club! But at the end of the day, I wasn't taught how to make this happen.

Here's why I am so grateful for having had this valley in our life.

I remember soon after the Walmart experience, I made an intention and wrote in my journal that I wanted to find a way to build businesses virtually so that I could be available to my children AND have a fulfilling career. The other part of this was that I wanted to build out businesses with my experiences in leadership and identity development in mind.

Dennis and I had NO CLUE how this would all show up because at this time, he took a close to minimum wage teller position at a bank, created a side hustle local magazine to serve small businesses with his marketing hobby at that time, and I was a traveling therapist working with children in lower income family situations and in the school system. We were draining our savings and 401(k) to make ends meet, and by December 2008 we were about two months away from losing our home.

Surrender Was The Answer

I will never forget the moment that we both got on our knees to surrender this situation. We had no clue how in the world we would be able to move forward and provide our daughter with the beautiful life we envisioned for her. My hands were high in the air as if I put all my burdens into my palms and handed them over to God. I was sobbing, feeling ashamed that I put our family in this situation while trying to better our lives with a side gig in direct sales that I hoped I could turn into a full-time job replacement.

We had no clue what else to do.

And sometimes, I learned in that moment... that is the answer.

Sometimes, we have to let go and stop trying to control the situation. Putting our intentions out there is powerful, and we have to trust that the intention we've been holding on to can happen once we surrender the HOW to get there.

In our case, that's exactly what happened. Around the time Maya was born Dennis also wanted to find a way to bring in extra money, so I encouraged him to go after this crazy hobby of his that he'd been studying since 1999 called Internet Marketing. I knew there was no harm in trying. All that could happen is that it wouldn't work.

Just a couple of years prior he had attended a marketing conference and met his mentor, David Frey of Marketing Best Practices, in person for the first time by accident in an elevator. They ended up talking for three hours, with David offering him a job in Houston, Texas. We weren't ready to move to Houston at that time because of our "steady" careers, but they had kept a great connection ever since.

Soon after our on-our-knees surrender moment with God, Dennis reached out to David for referrals of some of David's small business clients that might need implementation. David gave him two words: "No way."

We were shocked. What? Why not?

David went on to remind Dennis that he still had a job in Houston if he would be interested in moving his family to the area. Both sets of grandparents were in Orlando with us and it should have been a much harder decision than it was, but we were ready to own our journey and jump into business with an entrepreneur we respected.

One month later, we had renters for our home, sold EVERYTHING we weren't taking with us, and moved with our five-month-old to Houston. Dennis ran the marketing and operations for a new business idea: Telesummit Events, events created completely virtually and built over interviews with best-selling authors, speakers, and trainers to save people time and money, since we were deep in the Great Recession at that time.

Soon after we arrived, David invited me to be the voice of these events, and we grew the company to $2.5 million in just a couple of years. This was a side business for David but EVERYTHING for us. This helped launch my own company orchestrating virtual events for more than sixty coaches, entrepreneurs and visionaries, and led Dennis into a career where he is now seen as one of the world's best strategists in marketing operations for numerous well-known marketing brands and organizations.

After more than a decade of living a life as an entrepreneur, I've learned how to build out businesses that create and cultivate money from a place of joy. And using my gifts in leadership and identity development has led me to create four companies I'm very proud of: our virtual event management company; the business incubator known as The Tribe with Ryan Moran; Perky Perky Coffee; and my passion, to consult with 5- to 7-figure brands on how to build community-based business models effectively and profitably.

It also gave me the capacity and the capability to be more available to my daughter. Every Friday for the next four years, Maya and I would have a full day of play together. In essence, we would spend all day having quality time and enjoying the little and big moments of her going from a newborn and into toddlerhood. This was just the beginning of a new career for me, and it was so much more aligned than I ever could imagine.

When I placed that intention in 2008, I wanted to answer this question with everything in my being: "How can I invite leaders to show up and rise up, but do it virtually and do it in an out of the box way where I'm not sitting in an office day in and day out? How can I do that?"

What kept showing up for me was to trust this process, and it's now been twelve years that I've been doing so. At this point in my life, I have not just built and sold a virtual event management company, but I've also run a business incubator for e-commerce brands. I've built a coffee company that the

United Nations showcased on Women's Entrepreneurship Day as one of 10 brands to be on the lookout for in 2020.

I am creating a TV show in collaboration with a Cookie Company called Nunbelievable, which was co-founded by Tony Robbins. I've built a successful agency helping other business owners create communities in the way I've done over and over again.

Had I just focused on the belief that "life is hard," I can imagine that I wouldn't have given myself permission to see what else is possible, to enjoy work and life. Instead, I gave myself permission to see a new possibility by getting out of my own way and charting my own path.

It has been such a fantastic journey to craft a life based on intention and surrender. I put the intentions out there and then surrender the HOW it's going to show up. Instead, I focus on showing up for the journey — the lessons, the experiences, and the new opportunities that land because I choose to show up instead of a life that's built out of "shoulds," "musts," and fear.

I think it's also important to note that this is not done alone. Overcoming obstacles is not just a solo endeavor. Ever. This journey has been built on the fact that I've been open to my community, to friends and family giving their support in their own ways.

There's gonna be moments where we feel completely out of control. We don't see the other side. Even so, I believe that the power of surrender and the power of believing and living into our own magical and big adventure can be enough. If you allow yourself to be open to the possibility that your dreams are possible, that the intentions you have in your life are indeed possible... then and only then, will you have a chance to ACTUALLY create it.

My hope is that you start to share your dreams with people who you feel safe with to share those dreams and surround yourself with others who want to encourage you to create a new possibility. That is how you rise!

Maruxa Murphy is a Community Architect and serial entrepreneur looking to help businesses cultivate community and connection within and through their clients and customers; she has built more than three dozen communities over the last twenty years. When she's not building communities for others, she's enjoying time with her family in Central Florida, creating new possibilities in the intersection of entrepreneurship, education, and living life to the fullest.

MaruxaMurphy.com

CHAPTER NINE

Perspective Shift

Dr. Melissa Peet

As I stood in my dark kitchen, lit only by the bulb that turned on when I opened my empty refrigerator, tidal waves of shame rushed through me. Between attending my own graduate-level courses and teaching undergraduates all week at the University of Michigan, I'd somehow managed to work seventy hours over six days and had nothing fresh or healthy to feed Isaiah, my ten-year-old son. Thank god he was willing to eat anything, including another package of cheap ramen noodles with a few eggs thrown in, an entire meal for less than 75 cents.

We'd run out of food stamps for the month a few days before, so there was nothing left but stacks of those cheap brittle noodles and the chemical flavor packets that made them edible. As I poured the hot water over the noodles, my hand began to shake, my mouth went dry, and my heart pounded loudly in my ears. Panic was setting in, flooding me with all the questions I worked so hard to keep at bay: How am I going to make rent, get more food, or pay the fees for Isaiah to go to basketball camp next week?

The only thing worse than the anxiety was the burning shame I felt in every cell of my body – Am I on the right path? Should I be doing something else? How come I'm so broke? These questions felt crushing, especially now, at the end of one of the worst days I've ever had.

Up to that day, I kept the despair at bay by telling myself I was a good mom because I'd made a point to be home with Isaiah after I picked him up from school each day. The hours between 4:00 and 8:30 were ours; they were our sacred time. I loved our routine: we'd come home, turn on reruns of Xena Warrior Princess on TV and camp out on either end of the couch for thirty minutes. While he received a healthy dose of buxom women's empowerment, I took a power nap. After Xena ended, we'd do homework, hang out, play some games, and make dinner. Being Isaiah's mom was the highlight of my life. Nothing else came close.

After he went to bed around 8:30 or 9:00, I'd stay up past midnight, get a few hours of sleep, and then be back up around 5 a.m. And we'd do it again the next day. I spent nearly a decade on four hours of sleep, living mostly on caffeine and adrenaline.

I didn't have a rational reason why I was so compelled to get a pile of academic degrees: first a BA in Japanese language, then a master's in social work, and now, trudging towards a PhD in higher education. I was a first-generation college student, which means I had no internal compass and even fewer instincts when it came to playing the academic game. Thus, I'd stopped and started quite a few times while getting my degrees. I'd been at it for fourteen years and counting. I was exhausted from the long journey, bone tired of being poor, but I couldn't imagine doing anything else.

My meager "career plan" consisted of a simple daily ritual: Each morning, I'd get on my knees, put my head on the ground, and ask some Creator of the Universe, "Please show me what I'm supposed to do today and give me the strength to do it. " Inevitably, the answer that came back to me was, "Get your PhD." So that's what I was doing. I was simply following what the voice told me to do. It didn't make a damn bit of sense to me.

I loved teaching and doing research. I had a mind that could make sense of massive amounts of incoherent data and information, as long as it was about a topic that held my interest. I could find hidden threads within vast complexity. I liked to argue, and I was good at it. But these capacities didn't amount to a purpose, or a sense of direction, or a vision. I had skills but no intrinsic desire to be an academic.

Thus, I walked in faith each day because the alternative — absolute terror and despair — was far worse.

I took a few slow breaths as I prepared Isaiah's noodles, begging myself to calm down.

Crossroads, And A Discovery

After three years of grinding through my PhD coursework, hustling two or three jobs along the way (teacher, waitress, diversity trainer, etc.), I was finally at a crossroads: it was time to do my preliminary exams, a one-hundred-page paper based on a series of research questions. In our department, "prelims" were a gauntlet, held once a year, and intended to weed out the intellectually weak. If I passed the eight-week exam, I'd be free to go on to the final stage of my PhD program — doing original research and writing my dissertation. If I failed, then I'd be kicked out of the program and the previous three years would've been a total waste.

It was time to get past the prelim hump.

The only problem was that I was totally unprepared: while my childless peers had spent the previous two years honing their research questions and getting hundreds of academic resources lined up and ready to go, I'd done absolutely nothing to prepare. Zilch. I had no time. Just getting through my coursework felt like a miraculous feat.

But my lack of academic preparation was nothing compared to the financial challenge I faced: In order to spend eighty hours a week doing my prelims, I'd have to stop working, at least for the summer. But if I did that, I'd have no way to pay for rent, food, or anything else we needed. I couldn't afford any more student loans. I was maxed out.

"How do other people in my program manage this?" I thought.

That's when I started paying much closer attention to my peers for the first time. There were about a dozen of us in my cohort. I was particularly interested in the white men because I didn't perceive them as struggling nearly as much as everyone else (especially me) and I wanted to know why. As the only single mother in my PhD program, I'd never had time to hang out, socialize, or get to know my peers. I talked to them in class but that was it.

The first one I pulled aside was Tim – he was a year ahead of me and already through his prelims. Over coffee, I asked where he worked, how he paid for graduate school, how many hours he spent on his prelims, etc.

What I learned shocked me. Tim was a research assistant fifteen hours a week for one of the most productive "famous" faculty in our department. That was his only job, and in return for those fifteen hours, he was given a hefty "funding package" that paid for tuition, health care, and a monthly stipend for rent and food.

"What? How did you get that?" I asked.

"They offered it to me when they accepted me into the program."

No such package was ever offered to me.

While I was hustling day and night, Tim was being paid to learn. No wonder he seemed less stressed.

As I soon learned, Tim was not the only one. I spoke with at least a half dozen of my peers who had similar funding packages. I'd had no idea.

How did they come by this support? How come it was never offered to me? The more I asked, the more the disparity became clear: those who received support packages were also assigned to work with the most productive and successful faculty. Thus, not only were they able to eat and pay their bills without worry of homelessness, they were also getting a level of mentoring and guidance that was beyond my wildest dreams. By the time they completed the program, they were well published, got top-notch jobs and were "set" for their careers.

I was in shock.

I wasn't getting any support – personally, financially, or academically — from my department, and worst of all, I didn't even know that I could have. I felt like a complete idiot.

My first thought was that it must be some kind of mistake, an administrative snafu. Something must have gotten lost at the beginning of the program and that's how this inequality started.

I just needed to go talk to someone and let them know about it.

So off to the dean's office I went.

"Hi, I'm here to see dean_____"

"OK, what would you like to see her for?" asked the office manager who greeted me.

"Um... well, I need to do my prelims in a few weeks, I'm a single mom, and I can't figure out how to do them because I don't have any funding... but my peers are fully funded and so I need some support too, at least for the summer.."

Before I could finish my plea, she interrupted me with a rather sharp and dismissive tone: "Well, there's nothing we can do to help you. You should've thought about that before you came here."

"Huh? What?"

"We can't help you. Funding is based on merit. Clearly, if they'd seen you as worthy of funding when you came here, they would have given it to you. You should've thought through all this before you even said 'yes' to the program in the first place."

My head was spinning, the room tilted. "But wait, wait, what do you mean, merit? I mean, I can't complete my PhD program without at least SOME funding to get through the summer. I can't go on... "

"That's not our problem, you should've thought about that three years ago."

"Huh? Are you serious?" I asked.

"Yes," she said as she intentionally looked away.

"OK, Um... when you say 'merit,' what does that mean?"

"You'll have to discuss that with someone in your department." And then she shook her head with disgust and walked away.

As I stood in the hallway outside the dean's office, my chest felt tight and it hurt to breathe. I made my way to a nearby corner, slid down the cold green-tiled wall, and sat on the floor for a while. Shame washed through every cell of my being: I had somehow been deemed fundamentally less valuable than all of my peers and I didn't even know it. I wasn't worthy of investment and they were. How did I miss this? How did I not know? What's wrong with me?

I was being measured against criteria I didn't even know existed.

I was losing a game I didn't even know was being played.

I was missing out on a world of resources that I didn't even know existed.

While I was used to feeling like a complete imposter, I'd never felt so completely humiliated.

As I poured the hot water over Isaiah's brittle ramen noodles later that night, the words of the woman in the dean's office kept running through me in an endless loop: "You should have thought about that before you even started the program... "

I stirred the packet of seasonings into his bowl and took a bit of comfort in the fact that I felt too sick to eat, which meant we were one step closer to the ramen noodles lasting until the end of the month.

That night after Isiah went to bed, I didn't know what to do so I just laid on the garage-sale rug on my bedroom floor and pulled a blanket over me. I didn't feel like I belonged anywhere, not even in my own bed.

When I woke in the middle of the night, stiff with cold from sleeping on the floor, I was still filled with shock and despair. So I did the only thing I knew to do — I rolled over onto my knees, put my face in my hands, and rested my head on the floor and prayed, "Please show me what to do and give me the strength to do it... "

As I spoke those words, the tightening in my chest grabbed hold again, squeezing the air out of my lungs. I gasped for air and then it felt like a dam broke inside of me. Years of holding myself together broke free. I sobbed and sobbed, soaking my green shag rug with tears.

"I'm not getting up until you show me what to do" I said to whomever was listening, and then I resumed the fetal position and went back to sleep.

A few hours later the light outside my window creeped in. Morning had come. I needed to get Isaiah to school. I got up even though I still had no idea what to do.

A Shift In Focus

As I put a heap of leftover oatmeal in a pan on the stove, I heard a voice within me shout: "Stop taking it so personally! Whatever is happening, it is a structural issue. The University of Michigan is an institution, a system. You need to look at this institutionally, NOT as an individual failure."

Because structural inequality and systemic racism were topics I readily taught my students, the instruction to "look at this institutionally" made perfect sense to me.

After I dropped Isaiah off at school, I sent my academic advisor, a faculty member in my department, an urgent email message: "I need to see you as soon as possible." I wasn't sure what I was going to say or how she could help, I just knew I needed to talk with her.

By the time I entered the School of Education later that morning, my tears were gone. As I walked down the hallway toward my advisor's office, anger and certitude washed over me. I became incredibly calm. My legs felt like tree trunks as I walked.

I told her about the conversation I'd had with the woman in the dean's office. She empathized.

"What merit is she referring to and how is it measured?" I asked. "What do they have that I don't?"

While my voice was completely calm, the energy I exuded conveyed that I was no longer willing to be a participant in whatever system had brought me to this moment.

"I don't really know," she said. "Their funding packages were based on criteria set three years ago. I was relatively new then. I'm not sure I was part of that decision-making process. We don't really have 'set' criteria. It sort of changes year by year."

"But if there's no criteria, then how can they make decisions? Merit implies there is some kind of objective standard – right?" I responded.

"Yes, I guess it does, but it's more complicated than that."

"Well", I continued, "My big realization this morning is that my lack of funding is no longer my personal problem. Rather, it is an institutional problem. It belongs to the University of Michigan. Thus, I am 100 percent committed to doing whatever I need to do in order to make the university aware of its problem."

"What do you mean?" she asked, looking rather nervous.

"Well, if funding is handed out based on merit, then the criteria for that merit needs to be shared; it needs to be made public."

Perhaps I imagined it, but it seemed like her face turned a bit pale as she listened to me. "You mean you want to make this public?"

"Yes, absolutely, I want to have a public conversation about it. I'd like to put my merit, including all the work I've done for the university the last three years on behalf of diversity, equity and inclusion, against everyone else's merit, especially the white men in the program, and see how we all measure up. If I come out even with them, then I think I should get fully funded too, just like they do. Don't you agree?"

She nodded her head slowly. "Yeah, that makes sense but it's more complicated than that."

"And since this is a publicly-funded institution," I continued, "the criteria for how a department spends hundreds of thousands of dollars each year should also be made public, right? Otherwise, it would be way too easy to discriminate."

She nodded again. "Yeah, that makes sense but again, things aren't that simple… "

"Whatever is happening here isn't right," I said. "It's not OK. It's a system where some people get funding and others don't — AND it looks like the people who are most likely to get funding are the ones who need it the least. If that's the case, then it needs to stop."

Again, she nodded slowly in agreement.

"Did you know that single mothers only account for .1 percent of all PhD students in the U.S.? If that's the case, then we're definitely an underrepresented group. And isn't the university spending millions of dollars right now fighting a Supreme Court case so they can have the right to make special allowances for students from under-represented groups?"

She stopped me. "So you might want to stop and think about what you're saying, and the kind of damage you could do to yourself professionally around here if you go about this the wrong way."

"If I don't get funding, I WON'T HAVE a professional life, which means I have nothing left to lose – NOTHING. That's why I'm willing to be as public and as political as necessary. That's why I'm willing to be as loud as I need to be in order to be heard. I don't know if you remember this about me, but I'm literally trained to be a community organizer and activist. I know how to make noise, how to shake up a system."

"OK, OK, OK I heard you." After a long pause, she added, "Please give me forty-eight hours and I'll see what I can do."

I don't remember much about those next forty-eight hours other than the fact that I was able to pay attention to Isaiah and sleep in my bed.

Crossing The Threshold

When I met with my advisor two days later, she was ecstatic.

"I think we have a miracle," she said.

In short, the university figured out a funding package for me that was equal to what Tim and others were getting. Additionally:

- An anonymous donor put $10,000 towards my massive student debt;
- The Dean of Rackham (the organizational entity that oversees all seventeen graduate schools at UM) decided to personally support me out of his own discretionary budget for up to four years while I completed my prelims and then throughout my dissertation research.
- I would be allowed to work as much as I wanted and whenever I want-

ed to (funding packages usually came with a limit on how many hours someone could work).

- Rackham was launching an investigation into how the School of Education was funding its students.

As I listened, it was immediately clear to me that my promise to be "as public and as political as necessary" in order to resolve this issue must have scared them. They were trying to make up for lost time.

I walked out of her office that day stunned. It went better than I could've possibly imagined. As I continued down the hallway and out of the building, a huge weight was lifted. It felt like I was crossing a threshold.

I'd never known what it was like to feel supported. For the first time in my life, I felt like I belonged, like I was meant to be someplace, and that I had a place in the world. I no longer felt like an imposter.

I went on to send Isaiah off to basketball camp and conduct original research for my dissertation. I earned my PhD four years later, and I never did experience professional repercussions for threatening to make some noise.

My life was transformed. And because I was able to focus wholeheartedly on my research, I made breakthroughs and discoveries that have in turn transformed the lives of tens of thousands of others.

I discovered how people can access the vast hidden reservoir of intelligence, strength, capacity, and purposefulness they already have. This innate "knowing," which I termed Generative Knowledge, is hidden from our conscious awareness — and explains why self-reflection so often falls short. We can only reflect on something if we are aware of it.

I speak and teach around the world and gave a TEDx talk in 2017. I founded the Generative Knowledge Institute, with a vision of ultimately teaching millions of people how to facilitate the highest and best in one another, and to use their knowledge to create positive change.

But I couldn't have done any of it if I hadn't gotten past my own shit first. Like so many other women, I was the blind recipient of institutional oppression and sexism — and I had internalized that oppression by feeling like a failure.

I was able to move past it by realizing the "shit" wasn't even mine to begin with. I got past my shit by dislodging it from my soul and handing it back to those who needed to be responsible for it.

Dr. Melissa Peet is the founder of Generative Knowledge Institute, where she leads powerful experiential workshops helping people discover and build upon their vast hidden sources of strength, intelligence, and purpose, and to use these resources to transform their relationships, schools, workplaces, and communities.

GenerativeKnowledge.com

CHAPTER TEN

Releasing More Than Weight

Kirsten Womack

My sophomore year in high school, I walked by two boys in my math class and heard them make a sound.

Boom, boom, boom.

It's amazing the things we hang onto. I graduated high school in 1981, and that story was buried somewhere inside of me for a long, long time.

It bubbled up when I finally learned how to let it go.

I've had a lot of things to release, weight being one of them. Exhaustion and illness being others. The weight didn't come off until I was ready mentally, physically, and financially. I don't want others to wait.

My journey has been a long one, and it's often been exhausting. The past thirteen years have tested me. A lifetime of carrying weight and stories around, a series of family tragedies... I was ready to give up. I was beaten. Fatigue, health scares, frustration — maybe I'd have to accept it as my normal.

But that's not what my family would want. They don't want their baby sister to be struggling, and the best way I could honor them was to keep them close to my heart and to keep that message to never give up.

A Series Of Health Challenges

In 2000 I was diagnosed with hypothyroidism after a personal trainer noticed I was more sore than is normal and suggested I get checked out. From the beginning, it was hard to get the medication regulated.

Fast forward to 2007. I noticed I was having tremors and that it was kind of hard to write. I was in line at the grocery store once and felt like I was going to collapse. But I mostly ignored the symptoms; I was working as a virtual assistant, plus my husband and I had properties and owned the Penn Avenue Mail Center, a UPS-type of store, so I was busy. That's all it was.

But others noticed. One of the workers at the store said, "Miss Kirsten, there's something wrong with you. Do you realize how much weight you have lost and that you always shake?"

About a week later I went to my mom's house. She took one look at me and said, "If I have to tell you one more time that something's wrong with you... You don't know how you look."

I thought I was just overextended — until the day came that I couldn't ignore my symptoms. I woke up with a red dot in my eye that kept getting bigger. My eye was burning and my vision wasn't right. A call to the doctor led to an emergency room visit; my eyeball had started to protrude.

I was in the middle of a thyroid storm, a life-threatening condition attributed to hyperthyroidism. I was diagnosed with Grave's Disease, which was attacking my eyes. And although my doctor was able to regulate my medication, it was still an up and down battle, bouncing back and forth between hyperthyroidism and hypothyroidism.

In 2011, I went to the Cleveland Clinic, where my doctor recommended a thyroidectomy. I didn't hesitate to say yes, let's do this. Something told me not to hesitate and that I didn't need to go home and think about it, I needed to just do it. Surgery was scheduled for the following week.

I'll never forget that first night. I woke up and the whole bed had a pool of sweat. The nurse said, "Honey, you've got to get up; we need to change the mattress. Sometimes this happens, but you're gonna be ok."

Something about the way he said it was different and stood out; it made me think something else was wrong with me.

Soon after I was released from the hospital, the doctor telephoned me and asked that I come into the clinic and said to bring my husband.

The doctor shared with us that I had thyroid cancer. Now I understood why I did not hesitate to proceed with the surgery. It was God in my ear saying have the surgery, don't hesitate.

I felt better for a short while, then noticed I was starting to gain a lot of weight. My stomach was getting bigger and bigger. People would ask me when my baby was due. Something else was now affecting my health.

A year after the thyroid cancer diagnosis, I had a new issue: a nine-pound fibroid tumor. I underwent a total hysterectomy.

All The While, Family Tragedy

I'm the baby of the family by a wide margin, the youngest of six. My only sister (there were four brothers) is the closest in age to me but is still ten years older.

My brother Kenny, nicknamed "Sweetsie," was diagnosed with schizophrenia and lived in a group home. He walked everywhere and rode a bike; his physical health as far as I knew was fine.

One day in 2009, Kenny stopped by his usual morning spot for coffee. He got the coffee, crossed the street, and dropped dead of a heart attack.

In 2013, we lost my mother. She was eighty-nine and had survived a quadruple bypass, five heart attacks, six or seven angioplasties, and a couple of strokes before a series of heart attacks and strokes finally took her.

And then, 2015. I lost two brothers within thirty days.

Tony had been very sick with several forms of cancer. He passed away April 6.

My brother Charles had heart disease, a defibrillator implanted, and was diagnosed with prostate cancer. He had a complication with his defibrillator and was scheduled to have surgery.

I was in Arizona at the time and looked up the night before the surgery to realize it was 9 p.m. — midnight his time. I called Charles and apologized for calling so late.

"I just wanted to tell you I love you," I said.

I was wishing him luck, but Charles let me know he was saying goodbye. And that he was at peace.

"I did all my favorite things today," he said. "I listened to Prince, had my favorite sandwich, saw friends... I know my body and I know I'm not going to make it."

Charles went into surgery and never woke up.

Time For Action, Time For Change

One night after Tony passed away but before Charles passed, I woke up in the middle of the night and said, *Ok, I've got this. I have to honor what they went through. I have to honor my family members and learn from what I saw happen to their health.*

I jumped out of bed and hopped on my computer and wrote about what was going on with my health, wanting to get the word out: you don't have to suffer, you don't have to be sick.

After Charles passed away, I knew — time to take action.

I enrolled in a wellness institute where I earned my Master Health Coach Certification. I was driven to help others avoid health issues.

Three long years after my thyroidectomy I finally got my thyroid regulation under control thanks to a naturopath in Arizona, but I was still fighting that beast of weight. I was fifty-five years old and tired of the never-ending battle to lose weight.

The negative self-talk wore me down as much as the weight. I felt like nobody would listen to me or take me seriously as a health coach because of the way I looked. No matter how much working out they saw me doing, no matter how much information I could give them, they're not going to believe me because I didn't look like what I was talking about.

The reflection in the mirror was saying something opposite of what I was doing. The reflection was saying, "She's not a health coach, she's not doing all the healthy things she speaks of. Look at her, she's fat."

I knew that I was an awesome health coach, but I also know how the world is. And that sometimes kept me from sharing more.

I also felt guilt. My husband Mack is a personal trainer and I felt like I was doing him a disservice. He's trying to help clients transition to a healthy lifestyle, and I felt like a drag on his business — he can't even get the weight off his wife.

Of course, Mack never said or thought that. He loved me regardless. He just didn't like that he couldn't solve this for me.

I was doing every possible thing I could and feeling defeated, and I had gotten to the point where I was just going to stop.

Then I remembered what I told myself when I was up in the middle of the night typing.

I'm the baby; they don't want their baby sister to be struggling. I have to keep my family members close to my heart and keep that message to never give up.

I kept going.

Then one day, I received a message from a Facebook friend, someone I really only knew because I had commented on photos of her dog. She asked when I was going to be a health coach with her.

Everyone has a miracle to sell you on Facebook, don't they? But I met with her anyway and learned about her program, which was far different than anything I had talked about or believed in before. I prayed about it before moving forward.

In 2019, at the age of fifty-six, I went through the program and finally lost the weight that I had carried around for too many years. I finally got to the root of why I'd gain weight back, learned how my body works, how the environment in which we live plays a huge role, and why I eat the way I eat.

More than that, the journey was about understanding I'm good enough and can have whatever in life I want to have. The program brings some things out that might not be so pretty — like my math class memory — but it really helps.

I'd been carrying so much shit around for fifty-five years. Had I not done this program, I would not have bought an RV and embarked on living a healthy lifestyle on the road. I feel so free.

I knew I was born to be a voice for women who are fighting weight issues. Women in their forties and fifties have experienced some of the same health issues and developed some of the same self-defeating thoughts and habits that I once had, so why shouldn't I walk hand-in-hand with them?

It's not too late. I urge women not to give up, no matter what. Keep trying until you find the answer. It can be exhausting at times. But if you open your heart and your mind, and allow yourself to get out of your own way, you can release the weight and live the healthy life you desire and deserve. Never give up on you!

After several years of battling health issues and losing family members due to poor health, Kirsten Womack discovered her God-given purpose: to educate others about how a positive mindset, healthy eating, and fitness are a form of illness prevention.

MoveWithMack.com

CHAPTER ELEVEN

No Regrets

Nicole Dean

Back in the '80s in small-town northern Wisconsin, a kid struggling with anxiety didn't have many options to get help.

I was in fifth grade, suffering from constant stomach aches — the physical manifestation of what I know today was anxiety. My parents took me to a doctor who told me I was going to have ulcers soon if I didn't stop stressing so much.

The prescription: everyone, including the doctors, told me to relax. And then they went on with their lives.

So rather than help in any way, the doctors just gave me another thing to worry about.

For months after that I panicked about the impending freaking ulcers that were doomed to take over my body and make me feel like even more of a freak than I already felt.

It actually became a joke in our family (to everyone but me) about how stressed I always was: "That's just how Nikki is."

That's how people handled a kid with anxiety back in the day. They didn't.

Out of necessity, I made up my own coping mechanisms over the years. Some healthy and practical. Others not so much. The stress was bad. I felt like a failure at not being able to handle life, and I slowly sunk into depression because of it.

Then the bottom fell out for me. My parents separated the week I graduated high school, and a couple of months later I went off to college. I sank pretty quickly and by the time I came home for winter break, my parents saw I wasn't doing well and made an appointment for me to talk to their counselor.

They were right. I wasn't doing well. In fact, the day before I was supposed to go to that appointment, I decided I was going to kill myself.

That decision was like a switch: all the stress disappeared and I was back to being me. I knew that the end of all of my struggles was in sight. The pain was going to be over soon. I walked around in a near state of elation.

My dad noticed but was confused. Yet, even though I was suddenly and inexplicably no longer depressed, he told me that I was going to go to that appointment. We walked in, the counselor chatted with us for a little bit, and then told my dad to take me straight to the hospital and to not stop anywhere along the way. You know, the kind of hospital where they take your shoelaces so you can't harm yourself with them. That kind. I suddenly felt really tired. Not sad. Not mad. At that point I felt completely numb and like my life belonged to someone else and I was just watching it happen.

I spent more than three weeks in the hospital, though my memory of it now is blurred. I remember we made crafts a lot and that I watched the comedy channel at night in my room. The food sucked, but I didn't care because nothing really brought me joy. And there were meds. It seemed like a lot of meds.

After those three weeks, I went back to college and tried to figure out "What next?" I changed my major to Psychology because I wanted to learn everything I could about how to be a "normal" person. Because in my mind, I obviously was not normal — since I just got locked up. I just figured that everyone else had the secret that I missed out on when I was born. At the end of my freshman year I also started dating the amazing guy who I'd wind up marrying. I had met Joe on my first day of college and he knew my whole story, was there through the hospitalization, and for some reason wasn't scared off by what I thought was my "crazy."

And again, I went on with my life. Learning what I could about how the brain works whenever I could. Still struggling at times, but at least now I had my Joe by my side.

Swapping One Issue For Another

Fast forward a bit: Joe became my husband, we moved to Portland, and we decided to start a family after my grad school plans didn't pan out as I thought they would.

After I had my son, the postpartum depression was unbearably bad, and I suspect there was also psychosis although I was never diagnosed. Because how do you go to a doctor and say the things that I saw and felt? I was too scared to admit it to anyone but Joe. And yet he was there. And he still loved me.

Once my hormones settled, something surprising happened: the worst depths of depression and the suicidal thoughts went away.

I knew exactly what happened. It was obvious every time I looked into my son's eyes. I went from feeling like I had nothing to live for — to suddenly having everything to lose.

I wasn't miraculously cured, though. As if a switch had again flipped, the depression and suicidal thoughts were mostly swapped for anxiety. What had previously been chronic but fairly manageable anxiety transformed into a sometimes debilitating fear, worry, and panic. If you're a parent, you know it feels like there's always something to worry about. Add anxiety, and it can become all-consuming. Fear and worry tend to be my constant state. (And as I'm about to share, I'm always using tools and techniques to make that my "used to be" rather than my future.)

The thing about having a constant state of fear is that you can know it's there and choose to do things anyway. Maybe it was all those years of finding coping mechanisms and sometimes plain old necessity — but I figured out how to feel the anxiety and keep doing. Because I had a child and a husband counting on me to be there and do things that needed doing.

As it does, life kept moving, so we had to keep moving, too. In September 2001, while I was nine months pregnant, I watched on tv with the rest of the world as the towers came down. My daughter was born a few days later. Shortly afterward, my husband's employer closed a bunch of departments in anticipation of holiday sales being slow – including my husband's department of more than three hundred people.

Practically overnight, we went from one really nice income to none, and from one child to two.

We were thankful that my Joe found another job, though he was gone twelve to sixteen hours a day, every day. And he was unhappy. And once again, my postpartum depression was not fun. I was constantly sick from the stress (fevers, laryngitis, thyroid, colds) and it was hard. Real hard.

Because of financial worries, I started looking at anything I could do to make money without having to put two kids in daycare, which was way too cost-prohibitive. We had a mortgage and our savings was very low.

I started looking online for ideas, but everything I ran across was scummy. It seemed like everything I found that mentioned working from home was a yucky site preying on desperate people.

So I decided to create my own site to provide real help to people like me. I wasn't an expert. But I didn't need to claim to be one. I just shared what I learned with others and they seemed to like that.

And here's the thing: Once it became essential for me to make some money for my family, the fear dissipated and I just buckled down to do what I had to do.

Because it suddenly wasn't about me. It was about them. And that was my first realization. I could do brave things without hesitation when it was about someone I cared about. I looked for other evidence of that in my life and I thought, "Well, hell. I'd run into a burning building if I had to save my son." That's brave. So that was when I knew I could use that as a tool.

In early 2004, WordPress hadn't become the standard yet, so my Joe hand-coded the first few pages of the site. When I wanted to publish a new article, I'd copy an old page and I would edit the content, which he showed me how to do in Adobe Dreamweaver. It took a lot of learning and HTML, but I figured it out. As I made my way from incompetent to competent, that helped my confidence grow. I started to write and publish and things took off pretty quickly and people were noticing.

I wrote about working from home and staying home with kids. I had a section on preschool themes and home organization and how to romance your husband, anything I was interested in writing about.

I made money mainly through Google AdSense and affiliate recommendations. I wasn't making a lot, but I could tell it was working. And I figured if I could make twelve cents in a day, then I could make twelve dollars in a day, and then I could make one-hundred dollars in a day. I just had to keep experimenting and creating.

You may have heard before that the mind likes what is familiar and it can throw up worry as protection when we face the unfamiliar. So the idea is to make the unfamiliar (hard thing) become familiar by recognizing that your mind is just trying to protect you — and doing the hard thing anyway.

So another trick I used during this time, while trying to make the hard stuff become familiar, was to look at every challenge like a puzzle. I love puzzles, so that made it easier for me to not freeze up. When I faced something I struggled with, I didn't call myself stupid and I didn't beat myself up. I was just solving a puzzle! Puzzles are supposed to be challenging, right? If they aren't and they are too simple, they can be just boring. Every puzzle I unlocked felt like a little more of my superpowers were also unlocked at the same time. And again, that became the evidence that I could do hard things.

About this time I met Kelly McCausey, who did a Work at Home Mom of the Year award. I was nominated and when the votes were submitted I won!

But here's where the anxiety showed up again: Kelly asked me to create a product. I had done several things other people hadn't and they wanted me to create courses to teach them how; I had published more than one-hundred articles on other sites and had gotten all kinds of traffic and exposure. Yet I had a complete and total block about actually teaching it. I mean, I just did stuff. I didn't know how to teach.

When I froze up, in typical Kelly fashion, she asked whether I wanted to co-create the course. I'd just have to show up and Kelly would ask the questions, pitch in some ideas, put it all together in her shopping cart, and I'd help promote it.

I took five seconds of courage and said yes. And then I went into freak-out mode.

This was in 2005. My daughter was so little, and I didn't trust her not to burst in. I was paranoid about being perfect and professional back then. I've since slayed that dragon, but I used to worry so much about not being perfect. When it was time for the call, I handed my daughter to Joe and put three locked doors between us — the bedroom door and two bathroom doors — and I sat on the bathroom floor next to the toilet, called in, and was like, "Ok, we got this."

I shook so hard during that call that I was sure everyone would hear it in my voice. But I did it. I did it with the help of my friends, which seems to be how I've done nearly everything great in my business. And that's when I decided that I was going to climb to the top with my friends by my side. Because that changed my business forever.

Saying Yes To No Regrets

A few major tricks help me do things I might let fear stop me from doing.

One is to keep my mantra in front of me: live a life with no regrets. When an opportunity shows up that is unfamiliar and maybe a little bit scary, I take a deep breath and ask, "Am I going to regret this if I say 'no'?" If the answer is yes (there will be regret), I agree to it quick. I commit fast. I do this in both business and also in my life. Whether it's going with a group to Italy for two weeks or walking into my first yoga class or buying my cute little Jeep, I always ask myself, "Will I regret this later if I don't do it?"

People are like, "Wow, you're so brave." They think that being brave means I have no fear, but that's not it at all. I just see it as me feeling the fear (because for most of my life I haven't had a way to turn it off), and evaluating what things will look like if I do something versus not do it... then taking a deep breath, going "Shit," saying yes and committing. Then it's game on.

So in my business, if I commit to someone, then I'm not going to back out. I may let myself down, but I won't let somebody else down. That's one of the ways I deal with fear. I just take a breath and commit to the scary thing. Then I figure out how I'm going to do it.

That's how I started going to events and conferences. In 2008, I knew I needed to go meet people in order to broaden my circles for myself and my clients, and the first event I considered was in Atlanta. I made a pact with a friend, another businesswoman, to go together and room together — so I did.

Once I got there, the first night we committed to leave our room, telling ourselves that we'd go down to the hotel bar area where everyone was gathering, have one drink together, and come back up. Once we got down there we met awesome people and stayed longer, but it's another trick I use that works. And I've met most of my best business friends since then by attending events. I can't imagine my life if I'd stayed scared and had missed out on having those friends in my life.

I didn't realize it at the time, but I was using Atomic Habits (which is a great book). In it, James Clear, the author, talks about agreeing to ridiculously small things in order to create habits that stick. He uses the example of committing to flossing behind just one tooth a day. It sounds silly but once you take action on that tiny habit, you continue to take action and usually floss more than one tooth. But that tiny commitment is what gets you started. Then momentum kicks in and you just do the thing. Promising I'd go downstairs for one drink was enough to get me to do the thing that I needed to do: Meet people.

I strongly believe that taking action (even baby steps) in the face of fear keeps opening doors. There are a lot of people who won't go to events because they are scared. I kept showing up and went to many. People got to know me and learn what I do. After attending a few events, I got asked to speak. I blinked twice, took a breath, and said 'yes.' And then commenced to freak out about it. You may notice a pattern here.

Public speaking for me is really hard, as I know it is for many people. I do the speaking engagements anyway, but I've figured out a strategy to handle the anxiety: I always ask for the Friday morning slot after the opening keynote. Otherwise, I find I'm not able to enjoy the weekend as much because it's hanging over my head the whole time. I let all the extroverts take the later spots.

I also think of what will make me feel safe so I can do the things that I want to do. With speaking, I prepare well, which helps. I have my outfit picked out with a backup as well. I kick off my shoes. And I find a friendly face in the audience who is smiling at me to focus on while I give my talk.

But the thing with anxiety is that there is not one tool that works every time. Not even for the same person. One day I may need a hammer and the next only a drill will work. I'm constantly filling my toolbox with more helpful things that I can use. And over the years, I can say that it's a BEAST of a toolbox and I'm still adding more tools.

My Business Toolbox

These are the other tools and tactics I use to keep moving...

In business, I have built-in accountability by partnering with others. I've done this off and on since that first project with Kelly. With my business partner Melissa at Coach Glue, I've got deliverables to take care of, so there's not an option to let her down or she doesn't make money. When I've hosted Beachpreneurs masterminds at the beach with Kelly, I couldn't imagine not showing up or helping her to fill them.

I also surround myself with service providers and team members who are very competent, and I treat them well, so they stick around. If I have questions, I know that they'll either know the answer or they'll know someone who does. And if neither is the case, then they can contact support to figure it out. I know they've got my back and I never need to stay stuck or stress about things because I have super smart people by my side.

I also ask myself a lot of leading questions. Recently I was feeling really overwhelmed with a project and I felt frozen on it. My brain and skin felt like they were on fire. I obviously wasn't making progress so I stepped away from my computer and closed my eyes and breathed. Then I asked myself, "What is the one thing I can do right now to move closer to this goal?"

And the answer was stupid simple (as it frequently is when we ask the right questions). One of my Virtual Assistants had recently retired and she handled a tool that I use in my business. I didn't feel competent using it. So I watched a tutorial and I followed the instructions step-by-step and the anxiety went away 100 percent. I just needed a little more prep to tackle what I needed to. To be clear, that was very focused learning, not learning as a way to procrastinate. But it was all I needed to move from paralyzed to productive.

I have another really effective way to deal with anxiety: I shine the spotlight on other people. That's always fun. A huge part of my business has been showing off my friends. It gives me a way to not feel like I have to know all the answers, and I happily put my ego aside and let other people be smart and brilliant.

I also ask clarifying questions when something feels unfamiliar and uncertain. Information helps me going into situations. Then I can relax and trust.

When I was invited on a mastermind trip to Costa Rica, I knew in my heart that I wanted to go, but I couldn't get past my worries to say "yes." So I got on the phone with the organizer and talked through all of my questions. Then I was ready to say "hell yes" and sign up.

My Personal Toolbox

While all of the above business tools are great and helpful, they aren't enough – at least for me. I have to address the personal side of things in order to stay out of paralysis and stay in productivity.

First and foremost, there's Joe. He listens. He gets me out of the house and into the fresh air, even if it's just to eat outside. He deals with some of the overwhelming stuff, too. He's unshakable when I feel broken. He's my constant. I have other friends who are also my foundation who I can turn to when I feel shaky. Find your people. They are out there.

I also rely upon daily self-care and daytime and nighttime rituals. I now understand that, if I start my day by jumping on the computer, fueled by caffeine, and then eat crazy so my blood sugar is all over the place, and then get stuck in traffic in a crazy long detour, then by the time I decide to unwind, my cortisol/ stress levels are spiked so high that they laugh at my cup of tea and essential oils like, "Sure... good luck with that."

Instead I do micro yet massive self-love all day long to keep my stress at a level where I stand a chance at keeping it under the panic line. So when I do get stuck in traffic in a crazy long detour, I'm not already in such an elevated state that I can't get through it. I'm calmer and might actually enjoy the extra time in the car – because I've chosen to keep that level more manageable throughout the day. Less spikes. More even. Usually. Optimally.

My micro self-love comes in many forms. Going on a little walk to my garden to see what's grown. A cup of tea. A few minutes of exercise after a bathroom break. Five minutes of chair yoga at my desk. A few breaths when I sit at the computer before I open it. Texting a friend. Washing my face with the good stuff that smells nice and just enjoying the process rather than rushing through it to get it over with. Just little things to remind myself that I have power to keep the anxiety from getting out of control. And keeping my levels more even throughout the day.

I seek to constantly learn more about how the brain works, I take courses on stress management, and I like to keep up on the latest science. Because anxiety is affecting all areas of my life, I feel like it's the one place that I can focus my energy that will have a cascading effect on all other areas.

Most people hate to hear it but I find that what I eat matters a lot. When I eat well, I do better. Plus I just think eating beautiful produce is an act of self-love and self-care that demonstrates to myself that I have value. That then spills over into other areas of my life.

Movement is also a huge thing for me. I once read that Harvard researcher and author John Ratey found "A bout of exercise is like taking a little bit of Prozac and a little bit of Ritalin." Meaning that it helps your mood and your focus. So I do it. Every day without fail. And if I get more anxiety, I do a little bit more exercise. Sometimes it's only a few minutes, but it's enough to flip the switch to feel like my body and brain can work together again. Even my son Mason will sometimes ask me, "Mom, have you been going to yoga?" When he left for the Navy he was worried about me, and he made me promise him that I would go to yoga three times a week. God, I love that young man.

As a fan of tiny habits, I've committed to one minute of meditation each day. Of course, once I actually sit down to meditate, I almost always end up doing five to twenty minutes.

I have such a great life and am so thankful for everything in it, yet the anxiety is always there. Of course, it's frustrating. But it will never stop me from living my best life and growing awesome businesses. The blessing from it is that it's allowed me to help my coaching clients and friends work through some of their blocks in a more compassionate way. I hope my story has inspired you to push through anxiety, fears, and doubt if that's holding you back as well.

You can do the brave things. Say "yes" and then figure it out. Pour micro self-love into your day. Every day. Small steps count! Surround yourself with supportive, amazing people. And keep doing awesome things. You've got this.

Nicole Dean educates and empowers entrepreneurs to leverage their businesses so they can live life with no regrets. And maybe we can even make the world a better place in the process.

NicoleontheNet.com

CHAPTER TWELVE

You're Never Too Old To Thrive

Hazel Palache

The first time I started taking control of my life was when I got divorced at forty-three. Unfortunately, during the following years, I took that control and used it in a way that made me less powerful.

I didn't know how to manage money or dating — I got married when I was nineteen, going from my parents' home to a husband. And until I got divorced, I never had to take care of myself. Consequently, I spent about eight years accumulating debt and going in and out of unhealthy relationships. I repeated this pattern of abuse and debt until I reached my fifties. Although I was learning, real emotional growth, I discovered, takes time.

It would have been easy to blame it all on my childhood, which was extremely traumatic and abusive — a father who was a rageaholic and compulsive gambler and my mother a battered wife. Just because people have a roof over their heads and food on the table doesn't mean that everything is hunky-dory.

For a very long time, as a result of the role modeling and mindset I learned from my drama-driven, highly dysfunctional background, I didn't lead a calm, positive, peaceful life. When you're abused as a child and grow up that way, most of your choices tend to come from a place of fear.

However, I wasn't going to wallow. Maybe my childhood was horrible, maybe my marriage had failed, but I wasn't going to remain stuck in either place. What I lacked in self-confidence I didn't lack in courage, which allowed me to keep moving forward.

Starting over at forty-three without a healthy mindset and the proper tools, I stumbled many times, but I was growing. I just didn't know enough yet to grow properly.

What I did know was that I had to move forward one step at a time. Even though I had operated out of fear throughout my life, I also knew there were times I had acted with courage and that I could call on that if need be.

Evidence Of Courage

I was born and raised in London and when I married at nineteen, I became the non-working partner of one of the largest eyelash manufacturers in the United Kingdom. I had my first child just before I was twenty-one.

In the 1960s, women didn't go out as sales reps on the road. However, it was also difficult for men to sell eyelashes, and that's where I came in. We didn't want to hire a team of women without knowing whether it would work. I had never been in sales before but I was game for the challenge.

I remember pacing up and down the sidewalk for twenty minutes outside the first business I approached before mustering up enough courage to go in. I may have been afraid, but there was also a part of me that wouldn't give in to that fear. Before long, I had opened accounts with many of London's largest and most prestigious stores. I became one of the first female sales reps in the UK, and because it worked we hired the first female team of sales reps in the UK.

I was also in my twenties when one of the scariest moments of my life happened. On a plane going to Switzerland, in the days before jet engines, we hit a horrendous storm and didn't think we were going to come out of that alive. When I was in my fifties, I experienced another close call on a plane traveling from New Orleans to California. We were the next to take off and were sitting on the runway when I smelled smoke, and a few seconds later everybody in the back of the plane started running forward. We were evacuated down the chutes. The plane's electrical system had caught fire and the plane wound up gutted. To this day I still don't like flying and avoid it if I can, but I will do it when necessary with a lot of positive self-talk.

I experienced plenty of fear when my then-husband and I moved our family across the world six times in five years. We bounced back and forth between London and Canada before finally making our last move to the United States in 1979.

It was extremely stressful. However, I was a wife and back then women followed what their husbands wanted them to do. I wasn't allowed to go to college because I was a woman and my job was to procreate, which is exactly what I did.

Still, divorce proved much more frightening than cold calls, near-death experiences, and criss-crossing the world. Getting divorced was the scariest thing I'd ever done; no one in my family would ever do that. I was petrified when I called my father to tell him. He responded by telling me I was bringing shame on the family. He wasn't interested in the fact that marriage counseling hadn't worked and I was really unhappy. He was only concerned about what people would think.

This was where I drew on the underlying courage. I wasn't about to give in to that fear or the guilt and I did it anyway.

The Best Was Yet To Come

Life wasn't easy after my divorce. I went into a lot of debt and I made some terrible mistakes when dating because not only did I pick men who were like my father, the relationships became like a drug. And due to what I later discovered was my neediness, once I got hooked, it became very challenging to let go; one of the relationships lasted for about four years.

For the better part of a decade, I had many lessons to learn: from bankruptcy to dealing with teenage addiction to getting a job and finally deciding my purpose in life was to help others. For a year I attended the Hypnosis Motivational Institute at night so I could get my certification as a clinical hypnotherapist. I also learned how to make better choices with men.

It took a long time for me to move from fear to confidence and by then I was just over

fifty years old. My fifties, strangely enough, was the best decade of my life. It was the most fun. It was when I did the most growing and the most learning and when I discovered how to fully tap into my intuition. That decade really helped me become the woman I am today.

Having taken many classes on psychology in my twenties, I was very familiar with the various forms of therapy. I also added a certification as a stress management counselor. After the year at the institute, I received my certification as a Master Clinical Hypnotherapist. The director of the institute invited me to become a staff member, which they had never done with a student.

About six months later, I decided I really wanted to work for myself and a well-respected local psychologist offered me an office in their practice.

Fortunately, I had a client in the entertainment industry who started telling people about the help she received from me. And I gained enough referrals from that one client to fill my practice within sixty days. I would sometimes work until ten o'clock at night; my clients' needs ran the gamut, from learning to have healthy relationships to reducing stress and anxiety, to healing their inner child from issues during childhood. In every case I used hypnosis because it allowed people to heal faster.

Success often goes hand-in-hand with challenges. A year after I opened my practice, I was driving to my office when someone jumped a red light and nearly killed me. My car was totaled and first responders thought I had broken my neck. It wasn't broken but I was left with three herniated cervical discs.

Two years later, I was diagnosed with fibromyalgia. Over the years this turned into spinal stenosis and chronic arthritis. Working with people one-to-one started to become a challenge, and I was getting migraines every day. Under a pain clinic's guidance, I gave myself daily shots.

I'd been in practice for more than five years and was in my mid-fifties. As much as I loved my clients, the pain I endured daily began to take a toll until I finally decided I just couldn't work that way anymore. But I really didn't want to give up helping people.

In 1997, I heard about coaching and learned that I could work with clients by phone.

I retrained and a year later I added certifications in coaching, neuro-linguistic programming (NLP), and timeline therapies.

You don't just close down a therapy practice overnight. It took me two years to finish working with existing clients, but I didn't wait to take the next steps. I started working with coaching clients at the same time I was winding down the practice.

Although I intended to become a personal development coach or life coach, which is what I do now, I accidentally became a business coach. I say "accidentally" because the people I attracted were women who came to me wanting to build a business but who were sabotaging themselves. So I not only taught them about business-building, but they also learned how to change their thinking and overcome self-limiting beliefs.

I continued to learn and still do. I took lots of classes and attended many conferences, often three-day events both in and out of state. I learned how to build a mailing list and how to give live presentations to a variety of groups. I was often interviewed on live radio, on teleconferences, and tele-summits. These days it's often on podcasts.

I helped many women build successful businesses because they changed their self-talk. Even though I worked with clients by phone, I always used hypnosis in order to make changes faster, provided the person was open to it. I don't remember anyone ever saying no. Hypnosis is just an extremely deep form of relaxation that allows me to connect with the subconscious area of the mind, which is where all messages, including self-limiting beliefs, are retained until someone changes the way they think.

As I got older and my business became more successful, I cut down to working three days a week. Today I can work with clients on Zoom or phone. If I know them or they're referred to me and they live locally, I will see them in my home office if they prefer.

Although I always worked in personal development, I was primarily known as a business coach for about twenty years. In 2017, when I was seventy-six, I changed the name of my business to Live Your Abundant Life and started working with clients who wanted to think more positively so they could grow emotionally.

My Philosophy

This year I turned seventy-nine. I'm still working because I love what I do, but people often say, "Are you nuts? It's not like you can't afford to retire."

My response: "If I retired, other than having more time for volunteer work, what would I do?"

I'm not a "Let's do lunch" person. I loathe shopping. I don't want to travel. When I lived in England, which at the time was part of Europe, it was easy to go to other countries. Although I still might like to see a couple, I've mostly seen all the places I want to.

People often ask me how I still have so much energy with fibromyalgia, three herniated discs in my neck, chronic arthritis throughout my body, and pain every day.

I decided a long time ago that I have a choice to think positively and live my life, and that's what I do.

Everyone has a choice. I'm not interested when people whine. If someone has a real problem and they need support and help, I'm there. Clients know that you don't come to me if you're just looking to be stroked. I'll love you and I will never judge you, but I won't just tell you what you want to hear. I can only help if people are willing to learn.

I really want women to understand that whatever they've been through, there's hope. You can walk through fear and you can create and achieve whatever you want in life. It's all about making choices.

I started my business when I was fifty-one. I wrote a book that became a best-seller when I was sixty-seven. I've had many challenges and have been through a lot of trauma in my life, but each one of those was a lesson that taught me how to be the woman I am today.

You are never too old, it's never too late, and you can achieve anything you want if you push back fear and put one foot in front of the other.

Hazel Palache holds certifications as a Success Coach, Clinical Hypnother-apist, NLP Practitioner, and Stress Management Counselor. She is also an Amazon best-selling author and motivational speaker. For nearly thirty years she has been a mindset expert, working with women over forty who are going through some kind of transition and want the next chapter of their life to be more fulfilling.

LiveYourAbundantLife.com

VAL SELBY | 113

Permission To Speak At Val Volume

Val Selby

Most of my friends and acquaintances would be surprised to learn how much I've battled with self-confidence issues. I put on an amazing show. I became an expert at covering it up and slapping a giant smile on my face and pulling out the humor. Not showing the hurt and letting the world think I was this badass gal who has all the confidence in the world.

Um, no.

I can sit and analyze the reasons I have confidence issues. I know one that wasn't intended to be negative but that I can't stop from popping into my head anytime my confidence fails. It's about the word "adequate."

I always excelled at sports. My dad often coached the teams I was on, and those he didn't coach, he was always my biggest fan and attended most events. I was damn good in three sports, in large part because of the extra conversation we had as we picked every play apart and discussed how I could improve. Which is normal conversation after a game or race.

Anytime I made a good play on the field or the court Dad would yell out the word "adequate" to me. Just typing the word makes me twitchy. He thought it was funny and I know he didn't mean it maliciously. It wasn't until much later that I realized how much it had affected me.

Dad had meant it to be motivational, as in, keep improving, but it turned into a word that to me symbolizes that I will never be good enough. It wasn't until my daughter was on the soccer field and he yelled it out to her that I realized what a trigger word it was. It's the only time I can remember feeling the need to stand up to my Dad as an adult. He's never used the word around me again.

I don't think me analyzing more why's will help me change my feelings of inadequacy. Recognizing the major one hasn't made the feeling of not being good enough go away. I don't think I want to analyze and find even more. Then what do I do with more of them floating in my head?

My inner critic had me convinced for decades that if I changed who I was, then I'd be better than adequate in that person's eyes. Unfortunately, that person I speak of... well that was whoever I was around. I was constantly filtering parts of my personality on and off depending on who I thought I'd offend or which group I wanted to fit in with.

I would sign up to help with things that I really didn't want to do out of obligation. I didn't want to be a disappointment. I "toned down" my behavior because it embarrassed people. I stopped dancing at weddings because for years I'd hear how crazy I was on the dance floor. Being me wasn't good enough and I constantly felt reminded of that.

The day when I woke up to the fact that I was changing who I was and how I acted based on who I was around is the day I finally gave myself permission to be me.

The Realization

We were at a gathering with really good friends. It wasn't long before I could feel "the look" from one of the guys when he walked into the house from the back patio. For anyone who's been told for decades they are too loud, you know that feeling. You know what they are going to say before you even turn around to see their face.

They could hear me outside, for goodness' sake. Why do I need to be so loud? Those were the words this time, but I could hear all the put-downs and little digs he'd said to me in front of the group over the years. They all rushed into my head.

I've been asked why I have to be so loud by quite a few people over my forty-seven years. But this time I felt what he said right down to my core. I didn't want to monitor myself. Why did I have to quiet down in a large group?! Dammit, I didn't want to filter my personality around friends anymore.

I shut down and wanted to leave the party. I had been having a great time talking to all of my friends. I had a lot of major changes happening in my life with kids graduating, a full hysterectomy, and the death of two parents. I had really needed the chatting to vent, commiserate, and ignore all that was going on for a couple of hours. I'd "let my hair down," which was why I was so loud.

I mistakenly thought I could just be me around people who I thought cared about me. Here he came to remind me that being me is not ok nor good enough. That I need to change me in order to fit in and be loved by those around me.

I retreated into myself and tried to be small. I wanted to leave, but hubby was having a good time out talking to the guys and I didn't want to bother him and drag him away. After all, it's not about me, right? Never about me. So I did what I trained myself to do and I changed my personality to please those around me. I stopped talking at all. I smiled, nodded, and listened instead of participating. I mentally vacated the party.

It wasn't long before the guy who told me how loud I was, was being even louder than I had been. This reminded me of a piece of life advice my mom had given me. Because of my lack of confidence and hurt feelings, I had never applied it to him in the past when he had put me down. My mom had told me that if something about a person really bothers you, take a look inward. Is it a character trait you don't like about yourself?

BOOM. Stop now and think about someone who drives you bonkers. What about their personality sets you off?

He had told me I was too loud because he is always too loud. He probably doesn't like that about himself. I bet he's also been told many times to chill out, shush, or any number of ways to quiet down that we loud people are scolded. Because he'd heard it, he formed the opinion that everyone should be quieter.

Owning My Choices

That party in 2017 was a pivotal moment in my life. I talked to hubby on the way home and told him what had happened and how I felt. This wasn't our first discussion on the topic, but it was one of our last. I recognized how I was not the only loud one at the party, but I was the one singled out because I was the easy target. I didn't argue back or even pretend to defend myself. I pretended to laugh it off when inside I wasn't laughing. I decided on that drive home that I was going to own the choices I was making.

But who was loud or not loud wasn't why I had the pivotal change. It was the fact that this time I woke up to how I let others make me feel. It was the fact that I let someone take away the fun I was having and the conversation I'd needed.

After that party, I realized I was pissed because I'm loud and that is a fact I'm not going to change, and I don't freaking want to anymore. I started deciding I have personality traits I like about myself. I took responsibility for making myself miserable by trying to change who I was for others. It was an eye-opener that I was living in an environment I created where I never felt like I could just be me.

It was also when I started paying attention to the idea that the people who love me, love me for the real me! Holy cow, what a concept. I've had friends, a spouse, and family love me knowing exactly who I've always been.

All the decades prior, they never asked me to change. Why was I giving random people in my life power over who I was? Why was I putting more value on their opinions than the people who had supported me through thick and thin for so long?

I realized that my boundaries were garbage and that's why people felt they could say or do anything around me or treat me poorly. By shutting up and making changes, I was telling them they were right, and I was wrong. Yes — at this point, I know we can all agree that these were not friends. Friends would have had my back when he commented, and they damn well would have noticed me shutting down. But I can't rabbit trail off to that topic. It's another good one. Once I gained confidence, I gained some kick-butt boundaries. I'm a lot happier for letting that crowd go from my life.

As I woke up to how I let others control my thoughts and feelings about myself, I started asking myself questions.

What is wrong with being loud?

Being loud has served me in many great ways. My favorite is being a sports mom and coach. No kid has ever said they couldn't hear me.

I can remember multiple times when my son was in football and wrestling and my hubby was laughing at me because I was coaching from the stands: "Hey, he can't hear you down there with his helmet or ear guards on." And the next play my son would do exactly what I said on the football field or his next move on the mat was what I told him.

BOOYAH for being loud.

Why did I feel I had to stop being loud?

I grew up in a loud family. Each generation in my family has one who is the loudest. I'm not it. It's a joke in my family about us women getting together in a room and the poor souls who marry us. They don't even try to get into the conversation. I grew up learning it was ok to be loud, even celebrated as a family connection.

Whose opinion did I value more about my being too loud?

On the way home from the event as I was recounting what happened, there wasn't a single time hubby agreed that I was too loud. There was no way I was going to take some jerk's words over someone who has loved me for decades.

Do I have volume control or am I out of control?

When a situation requires respectful volume, I know how to manage it. Weddings, funerals, and libraries are not listening to me at full Val volume. I am not rude or disrespectful. I am not being loud to be the center of attention. I am not purposefully being loud.

By going through the questions, I came to the conclusion that it was ok to be loud. Being loud is a part of my personality and it's pretty awesome. I come from a long line of loud women and we've freaking used it for amazing things in our little worlds. I became more than ok with being loud, and I realized it was a big part of me and I was ready to own what I can do with it.

But real change doesn't come just from recognizing it's needed. The revelation was awesome and pivotal, but it's what that moment set into motion that gave me power. Because I had smashed down and hid who I really was for so many decades, I'd completely lost myself.

I had finally given myself permission to be me. WHO THE HELL WAS THAT? More scariness as I stumbled through being ok with the many parts of my personality I'd tried hard to squash for years. The areas where I'd receive a comment or a look from someone and assume I wasn't good enough yet again.

Guess what happened when I decided, I mean truly decided, that it was ok to be too loud, too opinionated, talk too much?

I no longer felt inadequate. For once I was coming to terms with being ok with being me. Not only being ok being me, but wanting to be more of me. I wanted to share more of what I found out about myself.

This opened up my life to more things than I previously gave myself the ability to imagine. Gaining confidence about who I was, led to my ability to dream. Which led to wanting to realize those dreams. I had never considered traveling without my family. I had no idea I'd want to do public speaking or host a podcast. When I allowed myself to be who I was meant to be, I created a mindset where I didn't have to be good enough for anyone but myself. Since 2017, I've met many people who want to be around the real me.

All because some guy told me I was too loud and I finally woke up.

Val Selby coaches women over forty to find their confidence and grab unforgotten dreams. She uses humor and straight talk to encourage you to live as your best self.

YourBoldLife.com

CHAPTER FOURTEEN

Self-Confidence Doesn't Come From A Bottle

Tishia Lee

I had my first drink at thirteen, and though I forget the booze (vodka or rum, most likely), I still remember the feeling — how it warmed my insides and how my cheeks became flush. And I also remember exactly why I liked it, even though I hated the taste and wound up sick: I immediately felt like I had the courage to do anything I wanted.

When I drank, I wasn't insecure anymore.

Any self-hatred about my body or my looks — numbed. In middle school, I had noticed how the other girls I was playing sports with were way thinner than I was. A doctor told me I had an athletic build, that my thick thighs and broad shoulders were great for athletes. People would tell me I had such a pretty face, if I just lost some weight.

When I was older, a pastor said this: "If you lost weight, think of all the men who would be knocking down your door."

I was the first girl at school to have breasts, which meant the boys would comment and pick on me — but that was also the only way they paid attention to me instead of the skinny girls. So while it made me uncomfortable, I also liked it. I had formed an unhealthy connection between sex and love, spurred by insecurity combined with unwanted advances from a family member who assured me this was how they show love. When I tried to talk to anyone about it, I had been accused of wanting attention.

Alcohol made all of that disappear. For a while.

By my senior year of high school, drinking became a pretty regular thing, most weekends. The alcohol was liquid courage: I could say whatever I wanted, I could do whatever I wanted, I could throw my body around with the guys, and I didn't have a care in the world.

Until the next morning. Until *Oh shit, time for some damage control.*

But by the next weekend, I was back at it. In our small northern Michigan town, there were nineteen people in my high school graduating class and a whole lot of backcountry. The guys would drive their big trucks through the mud to a spot known as the B yards, a place the cops wouldn't generally head back to because it was too hard to reach. And we'd party there every weekend.

I started drinking cheap Boone's Farm wine my senior year — Strawberry Hill to be exact. One night I drank about three bottles of Boone's and probably should have gone to the hospital.

"Just throw up," one of the guys said, "and you'll have room." So I did.

When I left for college, the binge drinking escalated; I had my stomach pumped once. I also started having blackout episodes. I'd wake up the next morning not knowing how I had gotten there. But I thought that was normal. I thought that's how all college kids experienced drinking.

College is also when the drunk driving started. One night I was supposed to be the designated driver because I wasn't twenty-one yet and couldn't drink in bars. But we drank before going out — so this DD was drunk. I drove a group of friends into the city of Grand Rapids. I drove on the expressway. And I have no clue how I got us from that bar back to campus.

I had never wanted to go to college and was on academic probation almost from the get-go because all I wanted to do was party. I somehow lasted a year and a half before flunking out.

Like anyone who drives drunk, I did it a lot. And I thank God I never hurt anybody. The closest I got was a serious accident in which I nearly killed myself. I was lucky to be alive — which is the first thing the cop told my mom when he called her at three in the morning.

I had driven my Bronco over the center line, across the left side of the road, and into a ditch that had a cement culvert. The impact buckled the Bronco, and a jack in the back of the vehicle came hurtling toward the front, catching on a small tear in the back of the driver's seat and ripping it all the way down before lodging in the seat. Had the jack hit a little higher, it probably would have taken my head off.

I don't remember a thing about what happened before the ambulance arrived. My head was gashed and bleeding from hitting it on the steering wheel, and as the guy from the ambulance held my hand and talked to me, all I could ask him about was whether my Girbaud jeans and Calvin Klein shirt were going to be ruined.

I had some minor internal bleeding, no broken bones, a year's probation, and community service. No arrest. The crash put me out of commission for two or three weeks. As soon as I was feeling better and the blood in my urine cleared up, I was back out... and back behind the wheel.

Parenthood And Alcoholism

I was on probation while pregnant and a couple of times I drank more than I should have, but thankfully my son was born healthy. And thank God too that I had a family that was excited to have a baby around, and so willing to step up.

Almost every weekend it was, "Ok, what family member is taking my child for the weekend so I can go out and drink and party?" The first three years of my son's life, someone in my family took him for the weekend.

By my mid to late-thirties, I had started drinking daily. I'd wake up in the morning and crack open a beer because I was shaking so badly. I'd go through a six or 12-pack of beer and sometimes a fifth of vodka too, every day. I didn't want to eat because I needed to save room for alcohol. I was so drunk, so unreliable, that everything was falling apart. I was losing clients and business because even when I tried to work, I was messing it up.

My mother would call almost every day.

"How much did you drink yesterday?" she'd ask.

"Two drinks," I'd reply. "My first and my last."

I wonder now, did anyone really believe that?

As a single mom, I had always told my son that if he ever had a desire to live with his dad, to talk to me. At twelve, he came to me and said he did. It was heart-wrenching, the hardest thing ever to let him go. But our relationship was not good then — I was constantly yelling at him, and his father had settled down with someone.

So Caleb moved in with them at twelve, and I moved to a one-bedroom apartment in their town of Charlevoix, Michigan, to be nearby. His dad and I wrote up a custody agreement in which I would have Caleb every other weekend... which didn't happen often. Or when it did, he'd go to a friend's house and I'd go out.

Vodka was my drink of choice then. I could drink it and no one would know. I'd put it in my thermos for football or basketball games. Or I'd attend an event and even if I wasn't drunk at it, it wasn't uncommon for me to have been drinking leading up to it.

Turning Point

It was the morning after my thirty-fifth or thirty-sixth birthday. I woke up and there was a man lying in bed next to me. He wasn't even a stranger; usually it was strange men who I met at the bar. This was a guy I'd gone to school with, even dated his brother.

For whatever reason, as he lay there asleep, I started sobbing. I couldn't live like this anymore. I was down to almost no clients in my VA business and couldn't pay the bills. My son was pulling away from me. I was so out of control the night of my best friend's wedding that I had gotten kicked out. My sister had dealt with me some weekends when it was so bad that I peed myself. I was a mean drunk. People were starting to wash their hands of me.

I can't live like this. My life is falling apart and I don't have people on my side anymore.

The only thing I could think about was, I either need help to get my shit together, or I'm killing myself. Because I can't live like this anymore.

After the guy finally woke up and left, I made some calls. I got into outpatient alcohol addiction treatment and went to my first Alcoholics Anonymous meeting that night. For the first time in my life, I sat there and thought, "I'm surrounded by people who get me. I don't have to pretend to be somebody I'm not." I stayed for the next meeting.

Then my friends were texting. So guess where I headed after that second meeting?

A couple of weeks later, I took a family vacation to Florida. It was perfect: we were right by the ocean so the family would go to the beach and I'd hang at the bar by the pool.

As we drove back to Michigan, I was having an internal battle. *Not that long ago, you woke up sobbing; either get your ass back into AA, or you're going to continue living this way and either kill yourself with alcohol or take your own life.*

I attended a meeting the next day and stopped drinking. It worked for a while.

Relapse

One of the first things you learn in AA is that a relapse doesn't just happen. It starts in your head before the actual relapse occurs.

I was one month and six days away from my two-year sobriety anniversary when some friends who were coming to town invited me to meet up at a bar. The invite came three weeks ahead of time.

The relapse starts in your head first. I knew I had to share this information with my sponsor or the girls at AA. Instead I started thinking, "I've got this. I can have just one drink; I'll be ok."

I didn't tell anybody that I was going to the bar. I didn't talk to my sponsor and I didn't do the steps. The night came and my son said, "Mom, I don't think it's a good idea for you to go to the bar."

"It's ok, I'm not going to drink," I lied.

I met my friends and for the first fifteen or twenty minutes, it was all about me and my journey in AA and being sober. And then they let me order a drink.

As soon as I took that first sip of alcohol, it was just like I was thirteen again, and taking that first drink. I loved the way it instantly warmed my insides. I felt my cheeks flush. It was like an adrenaline rush. It hit me and I was ready to go.

The waitress couldn't bring me drinks fast enough. She'd set one down and as she walked away, I needed another. I was ordering two at a time. And then I drove to another bar about twenty-five minutes away to meet some other friends who had asked if I wanted to come out. Hell, yeah!

A cop followed me from the town I was in to the one I drove to, went into the bar I went into, and talked to the group I was with. The bartender didn't end up serving me. And I wasn't arrested.

I lied to my son so much that night. He texted and checked in with me so many times.

"Just want to know, Mom, are you ok?

"Yeah, I'm good. I'm not drinking."

Caleb wound up at the relative's house I ended up at that night. I have no idea what he saw because I don't know what happened. I woke up the next morning and the first thing in my head was, *Oh my God, my son. What did he see? What did he hear?*

I geared up for damage control and tried to talk to him.

"I need to apologize to you," I said.

And my sixteen-year-old son, already so well versed in alcoholism, looked at me.

"Mom," he said, "you don't owe me an apology. You need to apologize to yourself and call your sponsor."

One Of The Lucky Ones

Thankfully, I was only out in the drinking world for twenty-four hours. A lot of people who go out, don't come back in. I got ahold of my sponsor immediately and went back to AA meetings.

That was a turning point in my sobriety. A really small town is a really hard place to get sober. I realized that if I wanted to be serious and change things long-term, I needed to remove myself from the situation. So I moved more than three hours away, to southern Michigan, got involved with an AA program there, and got an amazing sponsor who called me out on my bullshit. I fully immersed myself in the recovery culture. I also moved into a house with friend and mentor Kelly McCausey for a time — and if you know Kelly, you know she would also call me out.

For a time after my relapse, I admittedly fed those quarters into the ass-kicking machine. But somebody at one of the meetings reminded me: I still had bits and pieces of the tools and resources. I lost my streak, but I didn't lose the things I had been picking up and learning.

And despite the distance from my son, our relationship was becoming amazing. After about a year he said, "Mom, I want you back up here."

That was it. I headed back.

I was really nervous about going back to the environment with all of my drinking friends. I knew I would see the bar where I was a regular on an almost daily basis. But I had a really good foundation under me after a year of working with that sponsor and doing a lot of the steps I hadn't done before. So although I was nervous, I also knew that if I immediately got into a program and reached out to the women friends I had made before, I was probably going to be ok.

And I was. Of course, there were a few times I wanted to go to a bar, but I stayed immersed in the recovery group. I kept my distance from the drinking buddies. Things felt different this time. Maybe it's because I had finally gotten honest with myself and done the inner work.

As of this writing, it's been more than six years since I've had a drink. I've moved to Washington State to live with my boyfriend of nearly four years, I'm building a business in body positivity, and have walked the runway as a plus-sized model. I love my body now.

I'm not as plugged in out here, but I do seek that interaction with addicts and have attended meetings. Someone asked me a couple of years ago, "You still go to those?" And my reply was that a diabetic doesn't stop giving themselves insulin. The meetings are like that to an alcoholic: something they receive to stay safe and healthy.

Today I'm thankful for being an alcoholic. Because of the program and getting sober, I'm living a life beyond my wildest imagination. None of it would have happened if I hadn't been an alcoholic and hit rock bottom. That started me on my journey of working on myself and becoming who I am as a person and the amazing woman I am today.

Tishia (Tish) Lee encourages women of all sizes to take up space confidently and comfortably with no apology. She knows if you don't take your space in the world, no one else can and that would be a damn shame.

ShiningSelf.com

CHAPTER FIFTEEN

Taming The Inner Critic

Janna Lynn Skroch

What the freak just happened?

I sat down in the office chair and asked myself again, "What the freak just happened?"

My heart was still pounding in my throat, I felt short of breath, my armpits were sweating bucket loads, and I felt dizzy and nauseous all at the same time.

I had just hung up the phone with my Realtor. The Realtor who I had been so excited to share my dreams and goals with. The Realtor who was within moments of presenting my offer on a building that I believed could and would change my life.

I sat dumbfounded for several minutes before waves of guilt, embarrassment, and self-ridicule began to wash over and through me, bringing me to the verge of being physically sick.

At forty-five, I was finally going to become a for-real business owner. And I had just thrown it away.

Up to that point I had worked for the same employer, a worldwide papermill, for twenty-five years. For the last five years I was the lead lab tester of a 10 million gallons-per-day wastewater treatment plant. The job required all shifts: days, nights, weekends, holidays. I was also raising five children with my husband and canning produce from our huge garden.

I had planned to step back from this crazy schedule by buying and running my own exercise studio. I'd always been interested in health and fitness, and felt I could do much better than the women's-only gyms that existed at the time.

Calming down just slightly, I wondered — Why, when freedom was within a fingertip's reach, did I throw it all away?

Surprisingly, I was way more curious about my mind's meltdown and my body's physical reaction than being upset about not buying my dream building. The overwhelming physical and mental reaction was way too profound to ignore. I had to find out what had caused such an intense physical and emotional reaction. In my entire life, I had never had a response like that.

I began reading every self-help personal growth book that I could find. I researched books written by "new thought" writers from the late 1800s and early 1900s, along with many authors who have picked up on that philosophy since then. (*The Master Key System by Charles F. Haanel; The Magic of Believing by Claude Bristol; The Secret of the Ages by Robert Collier; The Success Principles by Jack Canfield; Breaking the Habit of Being Yourself* by Dr Joe Dispenza; and many more.)

I learned about visualizing, responsibility, the right way to think... how all things originate in the mind and then are made into the physical. What we think about, we bring about.

I reflected on the many different ways I had tried but failed to start a business so I could finally be able to stay at home with my family.

First there was an attempt at an import/export business in the early 1980s. I bought the $300 kit complete with instruction manuals and contacts in China. The internet hadn't yet been born and snail mail was the only thing available.

I did my research, typed up some letters on branded letterhead paper, and sent them off to China. And I received answers from most of the companies I contacted, along with brochures, catalogs, and samples. There it all was — right in front of me. But I didn't do anything with it. It just lay there staring at me for weeks, then months, then finally after two years I threw it all away.

I had tried MLM (Multi-Level Marketing) business opportunities, specifically Shaklee and Amway. I was a devoted user of the products but I could never get myself to talk to anyone else about them. *I was petrified at the thought.*

I tried making different craft items to sell. I created a new way to string rugs on a giant three-foot-by-five-foot homemade loom and had an idea to sell a pre-packaged rug-making kit. It was fun and easy to make the rugs; heck, who wouldn't want one! Even the pre-teens would love it.

I thought this would finally be the thing that would allow me to make extra money and retire young. *But I didn't follow through with that idea, either.*

Then the fiasco with the Realtor happened. It was the eye-opener to the fact that I really had some sort of internal problem with pushing through and going into the unknown — getting out of my comfort zone.

I could never commit to taking the next step in any project that I started.

There was something holding me back; some fear that would grip me and throw me totally off my plans, goals, and dreams.

I reflected on all of the things I tried to do and how I'd sabotage myself when I got to a certain point. The invisible wall would come up with a neon orange Do Not Enter sign.

With this fresh realization, I knew I had to find the answer to why and/or what kept self-sabotaging my efforts to achieve my dream goals.

Getting In My Head

Why couldn't I make myself follow-up and complete anything I started? Was there a spiritual problem? A mental problem, stress, or just plain old lack of motivation? Do I really want to achieve the goal, or not?

Because of the amount of reading I'd been doing, I became interested in psycho-cybernetics. It's the science behind the way my thoughts create a chemical reaction in my brain and how the brain really likes to stay in its comfort zone, and how my brain would freak out and rebel when different thoughts created different chemical combinations in my brain and body.

That sneaky chemical cocktail would say to me, "You don't know the first thing about running an import business." "You're going to make a fool of yourself stumbling over your words talking about Amway/Shaklee." "You don't have any idea how to run any kind of business. You don't have the right education." "You don't know how to... "

That was it! According to my Inner Critic, I don't know how to do anything. And the really sad thing is, because I didn't know what I didn't know, I listened to it.

The Quest Begins — Who Am I?

I became aware that I am a Spirit having a human experience within a body, not a human body having a spiritual experience. I had heard this frequently, but I never really considered or attempted to understand what it really meant.

The saying, "When the student is ready, the teacher will appear" definitely applied to me.

An inner awareness was becoming present. Who was looking out through my physical eyes? Who was observing from the windows of my soul? Who was talking? Where do my thoughts originate? Who is that voice in my head and where is it coming from?

What was the Spirit all about? How could I learn to listen to the Voice in my head? A Voice that has been with me my whole life, and me not realizing the power that It has to create an incredible life for me.

A Presence that if listened to, can teach, guide, and reveal to me the answers I need to solve any issue.

I finally understood that the Me that I hear in my head and the Me that is looking out of my eyes is the co-creator of my life. My Spirit. My sweet, beautiful, and caring Inner Voice.

But there is another voice... the voice of the Inner Critic. The Inner Critic is also a part of the subconscious. The Inner Critic is the auto-pilot of my life. It continuously attempts to keep me in the comfort zone that I had unknowingly set up for myself.

I've dedicated my life to understanding the voice of the Inner Critic. How to talk to the Inner Critic in a way that assures it that my dream goals are on the other side of its comfort zone.

The feelings that I experienced because of this revelation ranged from awe and excitement to power and bliss. Sometimes my heart felt so connected to God. I could feel God's pure love for me radiate from my heart and fill my being. This would inevitably spill out in the way I talked with family, friends, and co-workers, and also in the way I did my work.

It's strange to think back on the care I would take in doing my lab work, my house chores, the gardening; the feeling of purpose and peace in doing these actions was blissful.

Changes

In 2012 the papermill that I had worked at for thirty years experienced a business-ending explosion. One person was killed in the explosion and hundreds lost their jobs.

I was fifty-two. I was now presented with the opportunity to build my life around finding and living my purpose.

I began gathering my thoughts around how the business-buying failure had been the tipping point for me and sparked my serious journey into personal growth. I've often used stories or analogies to help me make sense of things and give me a visual. How could I attach some kind of analogy to effectively convey the feelings I felt in those moments?

It was as though a rabid wolf had taken over my body and mind. It was devouring me from the inside out. And there was absolutely nothing I could do about it until I did what it wanted.

That was it! Yep, my favorite dog that morphs slowly into a raging wolf. It is trying to keep me out of what it thinks is a danger zone.

This analogy has helped me to win in so many different situations: business-building, health, and even bucket list fun.

Business: When I was starting my online retail business I had to contact a wholesaler of a product that I wanted to sell. I emailed them several times and didn't receive an answer. My deadline was looming and I knew I was going to have to call and talk to someone about setting up a wholesale account. Oh my Gawd!

Just like that, I was having flashbacks of the Realtor situation. The same feelings came up within me — but thankfully, I realized the wolf was attempting to keep me in its comfort zone. I knew I had to take action right then or I'd be dealing with another failed business attempt.

I wrote my script out, grabbed the phone before I could change my mind, and within ten minutes I had qualified to be a reseller of a very popular product. I've since gone on to be a very successful online retailer. I finally followed through.

Health: The dog/wolf analogy has also helped me to lose thirty pounds and keep it off. The scale didn't plummet straight down but it trended down consistently. I went from 180 to 150 pounds in about six months.

During my dieting (and continued maintenance) I noticed another character presenting itself: the sly fox. Its voice sounds like, "You can start again tomorrow" or "You can have one bite of that chocolate-covered, custard-filled long john," which happens to be my personal favorite pastry. Ah, I see you, foxy! I'd mentally tell it NO! Sit!

Bucket list fun: In 2018, at the age of fifty-nine, I started running chip-timed 5k races. Kind of slow at first, forty-two minutes for my first race. I've gradually worked my way to sub-thirty minutes.

Rarely have I missed more than a day here or there of running. I live in Minnesota, which doesn't have the best conditions for outdoor running during the winter. When the temperature was less than zero degrees Fahrenheit, the fox would tell me to skip it today. But I knew the next day would probably be just as cold or even colder. I told the fox to be quiet.

In May of 2020, I participated in a virtual half marathon (13.1 miles) and finished in under three hours. I love that I did this at my age.

I've gotta let you know that during the training and during the actual half marathon, the fox and wolf were trying to have some serious conversations in my head. "Oh my gawd! My feet are hurting so bad right now. Nobody will fault you for quitting. You've already run ten miles! WHAT ARE YOU TRYING TO PROVE?!"

I told them to shut up. Am I going to do the half marathon again? You know it! I loved it. It probably ranks among the top experiences I've had in my life.

I've been thinking... I have to share this. I need everyone to know that they can create their life on purpose and love doing it.

Uh-oh. The fox said, "That's really a stupid idea! People are going to think you're an idiot talking about a dog that turns into a fox that then turns into a wolf! You're not a teacher, who are you to... blah blah blah."

Oh, I see you foxy! SHUT UP!

So here I go. I figure if I can help at least one person change their life by teaching this analogy, I have to do it.

Janna Lynn Skroch is the founder of I Create My Life Today. She owns a successful e-commerce business and is excitedly creating an interactive workshop to teach others how to retrain their inner critic so they too can achieve their dream goals. She is the author of The Fear Workbook.

ICreateMyLifeToday.com

CHAPTER SIXTEEN

What If It Were Easy?

Melissa Brown

Life always felt like I was getting into the line at the store behind the person with the most difficult transactions. You know that person — the one with a full grocery cart in an express line. And looking back, all the tell-tale signs were always there. Yet despite the full cart with the distracted person pushing it, I ended up getting in that line anyway.

I ignored the signs and plopped myself in the most difficult paths time and again. And heaven forbid I give up and move to another line. That was not allowed in my life. I would not be a quitter.

Was it really just me, or was the Universe conspiring to make things more difficult at every turn in my life? Why did everything have to be so hard?

I bought into all of the clichés. The notion that nothing good comes without a struggle. *Hard* work pays off. Any job worth doing is worth doing well. Quitters never prosper.

It would be decades before I realized it didn't have to be that way. I could ask for what I wanted, and I could actually get it! I could even pivot and shake the proverbial Etch A Sketch and start all over again without feeling like a quitter or a loser.

Entering adulthood, I didn't see any of that as a possibility, though. Instead, I became the queen of making something different out of the lemons life served. It never occurred to me that I could ask for juicy watermelon water with mint and basil instead. No, I took the lemons life gave me and I struggled to turn them into what I wanted. Asking for what I wanted was unthinkable. I continued for many years to try to perform alchemy on lemons.

I used to hear people laugh when I told them how I made it through medical school. I would always say, "I did it the hard way, but I wouldn't recommend you do it like that." It never occurred to me that I could have done it an easier way.

I started medical school in the late '70s as a single mother, even though I was married at the time. This was when women were just being accepted into medical school, so when I was told I had a spot in the class starting the summer of 1978, there was no doubt in my mind I would be there on that first day of classes.

My husband wouldn't leave his job and move across the state where the school was located, so I packed up my ten-month-old daughter and we headed to medical school.

As if life wasn't difficult enough juggling a toddler and medical school, I also experienced housing discrimination. It was perfectly acceptable to exclude tenants with children back then and I could only find an apartment far outside the city. This increased my commute times to the school and hospitals. I also needed to find around-the-clock child care when I was on call during second- and third-year clinical rotations.

Once again, I found myself stuck in the slow-moving and more difficult lane in life. Because I didn't ask for what I wanted, I would have to do everything the "hard" way. It never occurred to me to defer starting medical school that first year when I had a ten-month old nursing child, moved alone to a new city where I knew no one, had no childcare, and no housing on the first day of classes.

When it was confirmed I was pregnant with my second child halfway through medical school, I never considered more than a short leave of absence before I jumped back into my clinical rotations. I accepted that my lot in life was to do things the hard way.

And boy, was I rewarded with more situations that were harder than they had to be! It was as if I manifested the most difficult scenarios with myself in the center, time and again.

I divorced my first husband, who I came to recognize was abusive and controlling. I had to plan my escape and move out of state secretly to start my new residency the summer after graduating medical school. I feared my ex would block me from leaving the state, and I did not want to give up the plans I'd set in motion for residency in another state.

Then, because I had taken some time off after the birth of my second daughter, I couldn't graduate in the spring with the rest of my class and start my residency in July, the traditional start time for all medical residency programs in the U.S. I could find only one training program that would allow me the flexibility to start residency later than everyone else. So I ended up in a New Jersey pediatric residency program instead of one of the specialties I desired. I told myself it would only be a year and then I would switch. I didn't realize that openings in a residency program rarely come along.

Although I couldn't visualize myself practicing pediatrics as a career, I stuck with the training for the entire program — three years. By then, I was re-married and due to deliver my third child towards the end of the residency program. I began to make plans for a career in pharmaceutical research after completing the training. I wanted a better lifestyle than what I observed from the community-practicing physicians, and working for corporate seemed the way to achieve it.

But when it came time, I didn't pick the "express lane" of life. I again picked the one that would prove to be just plain hard.

At the end of my residency, an established pediatrician offered to employ me for a year and allow me to take over the practice at the end of that year. In that same office building, a young female ob-gyn had built up a booming practice as one of the first female obstetricians in the area. She promised to send as many new patients as possible my way.

How could I not jump on this fortuitous opportunity? It looked like it was the perfect match. And so, in spite of the fact that I never really wanted to go into pediatrics or even practice clinical medicine, I found myself in pediatric solo clinical practice.

I was now potentially on call 24/7, 365 days a year. This was the exact opposite of a favorable lifestyle for a woman with three small children and a new husband.

All of these difficult circumstances felt like the norm. I didn't question why everything had to be so hard. I just kept my head down and kept going. Whatever life was gonna throw at me, I thought I could just absorb it and keep going.

I embraced things being hard and jumped right in. I tend to give my all when I commit to something. I found a coverage group of other solo practitioners so I could sign out when I needed a break. But being in a coverage group meant I would need to be available for all of these other doctors' practices when I took my turn on call.

It was exhausting. Mentally and physically grueling. The demands of motherhood and family were layered on top of this responsibility. As the years wore on, the practice grew. True to her word, the ob-gyn colleague in the building sent many families my way. I was soon unable to handle the daily load of patients and phone calls. I attempted to scale by hiring staff members to help but that wasn't the same as cloning myself since there was only so much nurses or medical assistants could do.

I suffered for years without asking for help from anyone. I eventually hired another doctor who would work towards partnership with me, but that didn't work out. Then I was suddenly left with more patients than two doctors could handle and only me to treat them all.

The demands of this large practice grew and took a toll on my physical and emotional wellbeing. I was chronically overtired. Depressed and snappy. I ached and hurt over my entire body. My skin broke out constantly and my gastrointestinal tract was chronically upset. I felt like I was falling apart physically... and I was.

I had brain fog and found it hard to think. Not a good place to be for a physician. I felt like I was on the verge of "losing it" frequently. I would cry but never let anyone see me crying. I felt anger but also felt I had to stuff it all in and not let it be known that I had these feelings. I stuffed down all of my emotions because I believed it wasn't professional to show emotions.

My days became quite robotic. I focused on just getting through them. One miserable day after another.

Once again, I found myself in the longest, slowest, most difficult lane in the line-up of life. Why did I always find myself in this hard place? I couldn't even take a breath to ask myself this question, let alone consider why it kept happening. Or how to reverse it.

I desperately longed for a solution to help me manage the workload and the stress I found myself in. I joined a large multi-specialty group that promised to manage the business side of the practice and I could just do what I did best — see and treat patients.

I hoped this would be my express lane to finally make things easy in my life. Unfortunately, it turned out instead to be one of the biggest mistakes of my career. After trying to make it work for five years, I gave notice and planned to go back into private practice on my own terms. I wanted to be able to practice the way I felt was best for my patients. Corporate medical practice didn't allow me to do that.

After some legal wrangling, I was able to get out of the contract with the group and re-establish a private practice in my town. The tragedy of September 11, 2001 hit at this exact time just across the Hudson River from where I lived in New Jersey. Several of the families in my practice were directly affected by the horrible events of that day. My doubts and my stress paled in comparison.

Soon, I began to question my decision to return to private practice. I attended an event called "The Chrysalis Convention," designed to help physicians explore their transferable skills and transition into another career. I came away from that weekend conference convinced that I only knew how to be a clinical physician, sure there was not one other thing in the entire world that I could successfully or easily do. I came home depressed.

I wasn't any happier being back in private practice this time around. On some level, I realized it would not get easier. I knew my health was being seriously affected and I needed to make myself my number one patient.

I decided not to try to make my career easier. I decided to give it up completely.

When people found out I was retiring from medicine, they told me they couldn't believe I would walk away from being a doctor. I heard things like, "You worked so hard to be a doctor." And I would shake my head and think, 'That's an understatement!' If they only knew!

This wasn't an easy decision but looking back, it was the best one. I've never regretted leaving medicine. I've never once wished I could reverse the decision.

It wasn't all fairy dust and rainbows once I walked out the door of my practice, though. I still felt physically ill. I suffered from brain fog, low energy, and upset stomach daily. I knew I needed to do some serious self-care.

I explored all sorts of alternative and complementary medicine. I immersed myself in many different healing modalities and suspended judgment as I explored them in an effort to feel better. In addition to working to restore my physical health, I consumed self-help books and programs to understand more about myself.

Along my journey, I was introduced to a life-coach training course. I enrolled in it, though not to learn how to become a life coach. Instead, I saw the value in learning the skills taught in the training and applying what I learned to my own life. Little did I know just how much this year-long program would literally change my world.

I'm now convinced that the difficulties I encountered, the way everything was so hard for me for so long, didn't have to be that way. No, the Universe had not conspired to make everything more difficult. My mindset and my attitude were responsible for the choices I made.

I examined old beliefs and operating systems with the tools I learned. I let go of being the victim. I released a long-held belief that everything had to be hard for it to *really* count. No longer do I believe that challenges and difficulties are my birthright.

Nowadays, eleven years after "quitting," I find myself asking, "What would it look like if this or that thing was easy?" I allow myself to ask for what I want, and I let go of the outcome. Asking is within my control. Not so with the outcome.

I've come to learn that the answer to what you want will always be no when you don't ask for it. With practice and mindfulness, it's becoming much easier for me to know what I want and to ask for it. I've asked for menu changes in restaurants and almost always, my request is granted. Airline upgrades, seat changes, perks that I never would have dreamed possible, have all been willingly granted. Simply because I asked. If the answer is no to one of my requests, I let it go.

No one needs to be stuck as the victim in the 'slow-moving frustrating checkout lane' of life anymore. Ask yourself the simple question, "What would it look like if this were easy?" The answer is there. Suspend the fear and the limiting belief that it's not possible to ask for what you want.

And take life one "ask" at a time.

Marketing Coach Melissa Brown shows how to save time and create great content that gets you found, without the anxiety of doing it all yourself.

CoachReadyContent.com

CHAPTER SEVENTEEN

Loosening The Grip On Fixed Mindset

Lynette Chandler

People are conditioned to think in terms of lack. It's one of the many things I've been trying to work through, and I half joke that I never realized just how messed up I was.

I moved to the United States about twenty years ago, traveling halfway across the world from Malaysia, where I was born and raised. At the time, I thought nothing of it. The majority of the world is pretty exposed to American culture, plus my family spoke English at home. My uncle was an English teacher and my parents were educated in English, back when the country was still a British colony.

How hard could this be?

I got here and it was like walking into a steel wall that you didn't even know existed. I had no idea there were so many nuances and that I would struggle so much with different terms. I was used to calling the trunk of a car the "boot," for example, or didn't realize people wouldn't understand what it means to get a lift from them.

Accents were another thing I wasn't prepared for. In our military community in North Carolina, it wasn't as difficult. But within my husband's family, I had a little more trouble with the southern accents among the nieces and nephews. It got easier, but I also realized, *Well Lynette, you're not all that you thought you were.*

I also realized how different our mindsets are culturally. Scarcity mindset exists around the globe, but it's a little more prevalent in some cultures than in others. I didn't even know that the idea of abundance was a thing.

I remember asking my mother for something, even something tiny, and every single time she'd say, "I don't have money for it." We weren't rich, and sure, she had to watch every penny. But once I became a parent, I learned, sometimes it's not because we don't have a dollar for candy. We tell our children we don't have money because we don't want to spend the money or we don't want them to have candy.

Our children don't necessarily know that, though. And if every time they ask for something, the standard answer of not having money is uttered, we pass on to them that we never have enough for anything big or small. Ever.

These days I catch myself more and more and try to be honest with them. If I don't want to spend the money or there's some other reason, I'll tell them so. Why is it so bad and so hard to be honest with our children? Sometimes, I encourage them to figure out different ways to earn or save to get what they want instead of simply saying, "We don't have the money" over and over until they think "Oh that's right. We're always lacking money, and there's very little we can do about it."

Mindset-wise, I have grown so much since getting off that plane on Feb. 19, 2000. I'm almost a direct opposite of the person I was twenty years ago... almost. We're always learning and I still have a ways to go.

It really boils down to growth mindset and fixed mindset. I was absolutely fixed in everything, to the point that if I couldn't be good at something, then I was never going to do it ever again. I had to be the best in everything.

If anybody else was better at doing something, that meant I was not good. I was second best and by that definition, I was worthless. This outlook also prevented me from understanding the concept of being happy for somebody else; it was never in my consciousness. My husband would come home and would be genuinely happy for a friend, and I would say, "Oh how nice," but it was lip service because I couldn't grasp the concept of it all.

I've pondered this a lot: was it really just me, or was it cultural? I've come to a conclusion that it's a combination.

I'm so thankful for my husband, who's been ever patient with me. Through our conversations and the way he would interact with me, through all kinds of situations, he taught me so much. Watching him is what spurs me to want to discover why he's like that and learn how I can be that way. My business interactions have reinforced what I've noticed in my husband and make me covet that kind of mindset and mentality even more.

Growing A Business

I've always had a desire to be in business, though I didn't recognize it at first. My grandfather has always been in business and from what I understand of his family history, they were business people in China at the turn of the twentieth century. Nobody ever said so, but I believe they left the country because the emerging ideology and politics then didn't bode well for their business.

My grandfather had a gas station that he passed on to his two elder sons, who built it up to be very successful. I remember visiting my grandfather and he would be in his office or outside managing things and seeing to customers' needs. It was fascinating to me.

He also had a certain freedom. At the time I didn't recognize it as freedom, but I knew he could come and go from work as he pleased while my parents couldn't. I didn't know what it was, I simply knew I wanted that.

Unfortunately, how to get there was unclear. It also didn't help that my mom, though I love her to pieces, has a lot of insecurities that got passed on to me.

My mom is a really good cook. One of her specialties is a type of condiment. People would ask her to make it for them and they'd reimburse the cost of ingredients. This food also takes a lot of work to make and I didn't think it was right she wasn't being paid for her time.

"Why don't you sell this for a profit?" I'd ask.

She would then give me all her reasons why she couldn't. Sadly, those reasons also became my reasons.

I didn't think I could ever be in business and on top of that, there were practical issues. In Malaysia, you don't just go out and start a business. There's a lot of paperwork and a lot of hoops to jump through. Most Americans don't understand how difficult it is for many people outside this country to start a business; I am so crazy thankful it's so easy in the States to get started and that I get this opportunity. I never take that for granted.

I worked for a time when I got out of school. I didn't have a degree because my family couldn't afford it, but I had gobs of ambition and managed to climb the ranks. When I left the country, I was a marketing executive for a Norwegian paint company and was being groomed to be the marketing manager for the southeast Asia region.

Then I married my husband and saw an opportunity to be on my own. The truth is, for the first four years, I didn't make jack as a "marketing consultant."

Much of it was because I was still so mired in the fixed mindset. I was this smarty-pants marketing person. I knew it all. I didn't think I needed to change anything or learn anything from anyone, I just thought I had to work harder. Wrong!

Once that failed, I tried different things. I worked for different clients, did some affiliate marketing, started a travel agency. Along the way, I learned I had technical skills and was pretty good with HTML. I'd answer people's questions all the time, then decided I could get paid to DO it. Thankfully, I also slowly began to shed my fixed mindset.

I started listening to advice. People suggested I teach others, so I did that. WordPress came out and I was really excited about it; one of my first full eCourses was teaching WordPress in 2004, not long after it was released.

I started to believe I am capable of learning new things and skills. So I taught myself how to code and moved from teaching to creating WordPress themes and then plugins.

For a number of years, I ran a profitable WordPress plugin business. After some time, I was burnt out on it. The pressure of a software business is pretty overwhelming. It made me irritable. Unhappy.

I started doodling and getting creative on the side. At the same time, my husband fell ill and couldn't work. There was a lot of upheaval in my life then. I grew increasingly unhappy with my plugin business. Drawing was an outlet. I also began to pray more and more for direction for my life.

I kept running into the ways and ideas to make a business out of these things I've been creating. But I resisted! I didn't want to do it at all. Part of it was because I didn't think anything I drew was good enough. Nobody wants this.

That old fixed mindset was rearing its ugly head. She kept saying, "You're no good at art. You either have it or you don't. Even your art teacher in school said you aren't good. Who do you think you are? Art is not like coding. You can't learn this stuff. Stop entertaining this crazy idea."

Getting rid of that mentality is a constant struggle and you have to be vigilant! You've got to learn to stand up to her, but that's half the battle. You've also got to learn to be brave and reach for the very thing she thinks you shouldn't be doing.

So I did and turned it into a successful new business and was able to let go of the plugins business. I'm happier. Much happier. Even my daughter told me, I am happier and a lot more fun to be with. That should warm any mom's heart.

More important to me, she's changed her mindset too. She's less moody. More optimistic about her future. Definitely shedding some of the fixed mindset that I had unintentionally passed on.

Success is different for everybody. I used to think success meant building a six-figure business, traveling the world, living like a rockstar. I'm not saying I don't reach for those. I do, but the less tightly I hold on to those, a strange thing happens — the more I am able to attain them.

Today, I value a healthy mindset so much more. This is definitely not by my own doing. My faith plays a big part. I am constantly being transformed. It's much less stressful and pays dividends in many other ways, like teaching my children priceless life lessons that they can pass on to their children and their children's children. A legacy that has nothing to do with money but everything to do with their humanity. That's how you change the world!

Another thing I learned is, just because you don't get over something in one year, two years, or three years, doesn't mean there's no hope for you. It just means the issue is stuck fast. It's really not anything about you, it's just that some things take longer.

The biggest relief for me throughout this is that I'm not worthless nor hopeless. I've been working on my mindset issues for close to twenty years and I'm still not done. Thankfully, I know now it's not because I am born like this with no hope of ever changing. It just means I have more work to do and truth be told, we all do till the day we breathe our last.

Lynette Chandler is a self-taught programmer and seasoned online marketer. In the last couple of years, she found she has a talent for design. Today, Lynette dedicates herself to creating beautiful workbooks and planner templates for coaches.

ThriveAnywhere.com

CHAPTER EIGHTEEN

Journey Through A Nightmare To A Dream

Nadine Rodriguez

As a bartender, I learned that the trick to talking to people is to let them do the talking. When anyone asked how I was doing, I would reply with a quick "Great" and then switch the conversation back to them.

The sad part is that I didn't just do this professionally — I also did it with my family and co-workers. In reality, I hated my life.

I was a few years out of college, bartending to earn money to pay off student loan debt while I built an online business on the side. The business was my dream. I knew I wanted to help people, and when I stumbled onto online marketing, I immediately knew that was it. I could contribute to the world by helping local businesses and entrepreneurs get seen online so their businesses could grow.

I'd had the dream of being an entrepreneur for as long as I could remember, and the quest started in earnest when I graduated from college, got a full-time job... and then hated it. I hated every full-time job I ever had, and everything about working in an office drove me crazy. It drove me mad being stuck in a cubicle under fluorescent lights, cutting my lunch short five minutes so I could punch in just in time.

I remember staring outside the window one summer, watching the landscaping crew and feeling jealous that they were outside working and not stuck in an office. I thought maybe it was the company, so I quit and went to a staffing agency, where I requested temporary work only. I figured I could work in a bunch of different places and maybe something would stick.

Every job I worked at, I was offered full-time work there. My friends thought I was crazy when I turned them all down. I just couldn't do it. It was all the same. I was stuck in an office while working for someone else.

Finally, I had a plan I loved: pay off my loans with bartending money — it was fast, easy money — and build a business on the side.

Around this same time, I met someone and got into a serious relationship. Everything started well, except that he didn't understand the dream I was going after.

That's when the fights began.

My boyfriend wanted me to get a regular 9-5 job. To appease him, I said that once my student loans were paid off, I would find a job. What I really intended to do was grow my online business so that I could quit bartending altogether and not have to work for anyone else.

I found a consolidation company that would help me pay the debt off fast. I just had to make an extra-large payment every month and they would be paid off in no time. Bartending was helping me make that enormous payment.

I also started plowing away at my business, offering my services to help entrepreneurs with their marketing. And although I got a few clients, they were terrible; they demanded a lot of work from me while not wanting to spend any money. I didn't (yet) know how I could find amazing clients and charge a premium.

As I was secretly building my business, my relationship with my boyfriend got worse. He was an alcoholic who loved to abuse me verbally, and I had no friends because my boyfriend convinced me they were terrible people who shouldn't be in my life. All I heard from him was that no one loved me, not my family or my friends. He was the only one who loved me.

Brainwashing is real.

Why didn't I leave him right away? I don't know. But I stayed for a few more years, and it got worse and worse and worse.

Because of the constant belittling, my self-esteem and self-worth went down the toilet. Every time I tried to market myself or do any activity with my business, I felt like a fraud. "Who do I think I am, trying to help other businesses?" was all that went through my mind.

I was also terrified of putting myself out there. What would everyone think of me?

My boyfriend's drinking and torment got worse. To escape the life I was living, I also started to drink every day. The worst part was that I was utterly alone in my suffering; I didn't tell one person about the abuse I was going through.

I hated my life, and I didn't think it could get any worse.

I was wrong.

Hitting Bottom

One day, I found out the company that was helping me with my student loans stole all of my money. Not one penny was paid towards my loans — they stole nearly $40,000.

I still had student loans, but now with interest and late fees added. Plus one angry boyfriend who said the cruelest things possible to a person.

"What else?" I thought. "What else could possibly go wrong in my life?"

The universe has a funny sense of humor. What you ask for you shall receive.

Next thing I knew, a sheriff visited and handed me a court summons. I was being sued for the loans that were never paid.

I wanted to die.

I looked at my life and all the dreams I had and thought there was no possible way I could achieve them.

How was I going to get myself out of this deep, dark hole?

I felt like the hole kept getting deeper every time I put my hands on the walls to climb out. I was sinking fast and saw no light.

This predicament left me completely broke. I had no savings and I needed a lawyer. My business was on halt because I needed to deal with this situation.

I went to the one person I didn't want to go to: my boyfriend. I borrowed money from him to help pay for a lawyer.

By then, I never saw him sober. He would drink all the time. In the morning, he was either still drunk or hungover, so he would have another drink to ease the pain.

I hated him. I wanted to leave the relationship, but I genuinely thought I was stuck with him forever. I remember I would watch people on social media boast about the relationships they were in. I couldn't take it and completely deleted all of my social media profiles. I knew this would hurt my non-existent business, but I was triggered by it.

I stopped watching romantic comedies and avoided anything that had to do with love. I didn't know I could leave him.

Months went by, and I worked like crazy. I picked up as many shifts as possible because I didn't want to go home.

In those months, I had stumbled upon some spirituality and Law of Attraction books. I dove in hard and started to see how I was the one manifesting my life.

With this new realization, I decided to leave him. I finally wanted out, and I told him.

The problem was that he was drunk 100 percent of the time, so I couldn't have a rational conversation with him. Every night I would "break up" with him.

Some nights he was all for it, agreeing we weren't right for each other. Those nights made me so happy... but by the morning he wouldn't remember the conversation because he'd been drunk.

I didn't leave at this point because he was helping me out financially. I couldn't survive without his help, and he made sure to tell me that all the time.

I got through my days by drinking and reading books on personal development. The books I read kept saying the same thing: I had the power in me to do whatever I wanted. I could change my life.

The seed that was planted in me started to blossom. I felt excited for the first time. I just needed to figure out what to do to leave the relationship.

Tipping Point

One beautiful summer night, I got home from attending a wedding with a friend. It was about 1 a.m. and my boyfriend wasn't home when I got there.

"Thank God," I thought.

He was supposed to attend the wedding with me, but at the last minute I told him I didn't want him to go and I went with a friend who was already attending.

As I started to unwind and get ready for bed, I was texting my friend to let her know I got home safely. I don't remember what she replied, but it made me laugh.

That's when I heard something fall inside the bathroom shower. When I went to check and moved the shower curtain, I found my boyfriend hiding in there. My shampoo bottle had fallen.

I screamed and ran out, and he chased me.

Because I didn't want him to come to the wedding with me, he thought I was cheating on him. So he hid his car down the street and then hid in the shower for hours because he didn't know when I was going to come home.

There were empty beer bottles in the shower.

When I laughed at the text message my friend had sent me, he assumed it was the guy I had been with.

That night was hell. He wanted me dead. He tried to throw me over our fifth-floor balcony to kill me. It was the first time the abuse got that physical. I've often wondered why the neighbors didn't call the cops.

I don't know how much time went by during our fight, but there was something inside of me that I hadn't felt in a long time: Hope.

If I survived the night, I was leaving him. That hope was the feeling of a new life — the life I was meant to live.

Finally, he calmed down and went to sleep. I didn't sleep much, though I was exhausted.

I awoke the next morning and went to my dad's. I was keeping the promise I made to myself. I told my father what I had been going through for the last few years and that I was done.

Free-ish

My boyfriend moved out the following weekend after I told him I had told everyone about him. He was no longer welcome in my family or family's house. Then I moved in with my brother.

I was free. It felt so good to be free. I was ready to fully embrace my life, start my business again, and have it explode.

There was one problem — I hated who I was.

I still hated my life. I had no money, I was living with my brother, I was still being sued, I had a ton of debt, and I was still bartending, which I also now hated.

My self-worth and love was gone. What I needed to do was repair and heal from the abuse I went through. But I hated being alone with myself, so I jumped into another relationship.

Except this relationship was fun. We laughed, we traveled, we were always on some kind of adventure. It was the perfect escape and the complete opposite of what I was used to.

When it came to my business, I thought I was ready to make it work. I hired a coach and was part of a group mastermind. I loved it, except I wasn't doing the work I was told to do. I absolutely refused to put myself out there. I just couldn't do it. There had to be another way.

All I kept thinking was what will everyone think, what will my family think, what will people from high school who I haven't seen or spoken to since high school think, what will my boyfriend think, what will his friends and family think, what will co-workers think, and so on.

I was stuck. Again I started to get into personal development. I listened to podcasts, read books, and listened to audiobooks. I was fully immersed and determined to make a personal change in my life.

I bought a few courses that helped me go more inward, and I started to meditate.

That's when I started to see the things that weren't aligned in my life. My boyfriend was one of them.

He's a great guy and was so sweet to me, but he was the escape that I needed, and he served that purpose. I was ready to move on.

So I did. The breakup was fast. I broke our lease and emptied the apartment in two days. With nothing left but a few boxes and my personal belongings, I moved in with my sister.

This time it was just me and my business. So I joined another group coaching program, telling myself I was fully committing and ready for amazingness to happen.

Yet I still held myself back. There was no way I could tell my story when I did everything I could to forget it. I felt like I couldn't show up and do what I needed to do because somehow my past would creep up and come out. That's what I didn't want to happen.

Because of that, my business didn't grow. I still had crappy clients, and I didn't feel like I was making an impact. Any type of success or positive thing that happened, I would self-sabotage it.

One day I booked a spontaneous trip to Southeast Asia. I needed to get out and see the world because I couldn't take it anymore. I hopped on a plane alone and backpacked through four countries for six weeks.

I had the time of my life. I met so many awesome people, got to immerse myself in other cultures fully, and I was far, far away from home. I loved it.

But then I ran out of money and had to go back. While my travel companions were continuing on their travel journey, I was in tears on a flight home.

That trip made me want my online business so bad. I saw other digital nomads make it work, and I had to make it work.

Letting Go And Watching Magic Happen

As I journaled about my life, I realized I still had to heal from my abuse. I had developed a terrible emotional eating habit and gained fifteen pounds, and it was getting worse.

I still didn't love myself, and I needed to change that.

I read Louise Hayes's books and programs, and I slowly let go of all the hurt I felt. I joined a mindset group that helped me process everything that I had suppressed, and for the first time in my life, I felt a heavy load lifted from my shoulders. I felt light and free.

I also realized I wanted my business for the wrong reasons — so I could make money and travel. That's nice, but I wasn't making an impact. It still felt like a job. I didn't love it.

As I kept healing myself, I saw that there were a lot of women out there struggling to build a business too. In all the groups I'm in, I heard women talk about their dreams, but they're stuck because of the same insecurities I faced.

My new mission became to help as many women as possible get out of their heads so they could have the business and life they dream of.

And that's when everything aligned perfectly. I love helping other women succeed, and I'm not afraid to tell my story anymore. If someone is judging me for being a high performer, for showing up and doing things to grow my business, that's fine. I accept it.

Once I fully let it all go and pushed my story and fear aside, that's when the magic started to happen.

I started to attract awesome people and opportunities into my life. I was quickly able to go out and make connections. I dove into my business like never before and started to attract dream clients.

It was all because I stopped identifying with my story. I chose to let it go and decided to rewrite my own and create a life I dreamed of.

It didn't happen overnight. It took work and dedication, especially mentally.

I still fell, but I was able to pick myself up and keep going because I had built momentum, and everything started to flow into my life. My dreams were coming true.

The one thing I learned is that self-love is the most important thing a person can have. Without it, all the insecurities come up.

But when you love yourself fully, no story, problem, or other people can get in the way. You become so secure in yourself and your purpose that all that other stuff becomes irrelevant.

Don't let whatever happened to you stop you from living your dreams. I would never change what happened because it helped turn me into a person I never thought I could become. You have the magic in you — dig deep, and you'll find it.

Nadine Rodriguez is a Success and Mindset Coach, NLP Practitioner, and hypnotherapist. Her mission is to help women overcome the limiting beliefs that hold them back from success so they can live the life of their dreams.

EvolveWithNadine.com

CHAPTER NINETEEN

Boombox

Karen Robinson

I ran away in the fall of ninth grade... and it changed my life for the better.

It's not that I wanted to run, but I didn't believe I had a choice. With no plan and no hesitation either, I packed a gym bag with necessities, grabbed my boombox, and out the door I went. I didn't look back. Somehow, even at fourteen years old, I understood that I deserved a better life.

Today, in my role as a licensed clinical social worker, I don't recommend teens run away. Yet there's also no denying that in my case, it worked.

Have you ever searched for articles on how adolescents can cope with their parents? I did this a year ago and found it upsetting and unjust. Most of the literature instead seems geared toward how parents can cope with their adolescents.

And while I understand that teens aren't angelic creatures with exceptional decision-making capabilities and that an adolescent's brain doesn't fully develop until the mid-twenties, I also experience that some teens live in homes with domestic violence, drug addiction, and/or many abuses.

Some abuse is gray (hard to prove), and thus they remain in homes with neglect, isolation, and fear. Can you guess what I say when I counsel teens in this gray area, those who don't have marks on their bodies but deep emotional wounds? I urge them not to give up. There is hope. When you leave your home after graduation, you can create the life you want to live. It won't be easy, but you can do it.

I understand a lot of what they're going through. Before I ran away, I attempted suicide. I took a large handful of Tylenol from a medium-sized bottle and washed it down with several swallows of water.

The next morning, I was angry to wake up instead of being dead. But as I reflected more, I realized God wanted me around; my prayer to die wasn't what God wanted for me. My faith background helped me find hope.

From early childhood, I would pray with my Grammy Grace and say the rosary with Grammy Lena. Their denominations were different (one Pentecostal and one Catholic) but both women had an enormous influence on my life. A woman named Van from church, who has since passed away, helped me with my first Communion and exemplified God's grace. And in that morning after my suicide attempt, my faith kept me going.

That was my only attempt. Prior to the overdose, I had stashed razor blades in the pockets of clothing I kept in the back of my closet in my tiny room in our dumpy little trailer in Rowena, NB, Canada. I never used any of them — blood grossed me out, plus I don't like pain. Besides, after I survived the overdose, I was pretty convinced that God needed me for something and I kept that belief, even on the darkest of days.

Because I never told my family, I never went to the hospital or saw a doctor, and they didn't call a counselor. Still, my mother either thought I looked depressed or she heard me crying, and she'd ask me what she should do to help me.

"Leave him," I would say. But she didn't.

Living With Trauma

I grew up convinced my father hated me.

Maybe if I had been a passive girl, he might not have been so reactive. He is misogynistic, while I was a feminist before I understood what that meant. I was born a feminist and knew that one gender is not better than the other.

I refused to serve him. I refused to clean up after him. I refused to pick up chicken bones from the table as he threw them down while eating. I refused to put his dishes in the sink. When I did comply and clean up after him, it was in order to wash dishes so my mother wouldn't come home from work and have more to do.

My father refused to work, and we lived well below the poverty line. He refused to buy food when he had money, so there was seldom food or lunch money. Mom broke all the windows in the trailer when he refused to buy windows with tax money. Our pipes would freeze frequently during the Canadian winters. The shower wouldn't work.

Toilet paper was scarce. Dishes, hair, and laundry were washed with cheap dishwashing liquid. We never vacationed. An enjoyable time was going to the dump to watch bears play.

My father idolized my brother and cursed at me. He cursed at mom as well and she gave it back to him. My father would often call my mother or me "bitch," "cunt," "whore," or "slut." The word "fuck" or "fucking" often punctuated his rants. The emotional abuse was intense.

And there was physical violence as well. I remember her hitting him with a broomstick across his knee and him throwing a plate against the wall. He was also physically abusive to me. He'd hit me with a belt, whip a bar of soap at me, or throw me down. I meant nothing to him and often wondered whether I would survive.

I lost my sight one time after he threw me twice — once at the front door and then into the kitchen stove. I'm not sure whether I blacked out. And while the vision loss didn't last long, it was scary.

He attempted to kill me once. He threw me to the ground near the woodpile, picked up a log, and was teetering towards my head. I closed my eyes waiting for impact. Mom stopped him when she picked up a log herself and hit him with it. She threatened him to never touch me again. She knows that she saved my life. The abuse didn't end, but he didn't try to kill me again.

I never considered that he sexually abused me until my child abuse classes in college. I learned that his attempts to get me to watch pornography with him were sexually abusive. He touched my breast once — a squeeze, and then he appeared ashamed. It almost made me sympathetic toward him, except I had hated him for a long time by that point.

How did my mother live like this? Oh right, she abused opioids. That's how she survived, and that's how I lost my mother most of my life. She struggled with depression and suicidal ideation. I wouldn't go to sleep some nights, worried that she would try to kill herself. I was in elementary school.

And then one day, Mom did leave him.

After I told my aunt we lacked food, my aunt called our family doctor to tell him to intervene. Our doctor told mom that if she didn't change our circumstances (lack of food and seasonally appropriate clothing like winter jackets and boots), he would need to report to social services, and she might lose her children.

So with my aunt's help, my mom, brother, and I moved into a little apartment in town (Perth-Andover, NB). I was over-the-moon happy, even though I shared a room with my mom. My aunt helped with needed furniture and groceries, and I could finally do things after school, like attend hockey games. My brother and I walked to the rink near our apartment. For the first time in my childhood, I was safe, happy, and secure.

It didn't last.

My father courted my mother again, and she let him. Dread. He promised my brother a snowmobile if my brother moved back home. I told mom there was nothing my father could offer me that would make me go back, and I meant it. She continued seeing him and the dread grew stronger. I was unsure what to do. I hoped she would stay away from him, though my intuition in the pit of my stomach sensed she wouldn't.

Running Away, Starting Anew

One day I came home from school and my mother informed me that we were moving back in with my father. I told her I wasn't going back and she insisted I was.

We volleyed — "Yes, you are" "No, I'm not" — until she screamed, "Why do you need to be such a bitch?"

We had been close, and her words cut me deep. I turned and walked away to our room and I heard her leave. In tears, I packed the gym bag and grabbed my boom box, then left the apartment without a plan, walking until I reached a phone booth.

I called two friends, who each asked their parents if I could stay at their places; neither set of parents wanted involvement with a runaway (I hold no judgment toward them). I then made a collect call to my Aunt Diane in Fort Fairfield, Maine. She really didn't have room in her home, but she took me in anyway.

Details are fuzzy. I remember meeting a case worker at social services sometime later. A friend who lived close by walked me there. The social worker accused me of doing drugs, sleeping around, and said I was a horrible teenager to my parents. It stunned me. I had never done drugs and I was a virgin. I was an excellent student.

Something in me changed. A fire was lit. Everything I had been through — child abuse, domestic violence, sexism, misogyny — it was too much. I decided: my career would help people. (For the record, if I had been promiscuous and abusing drugs, it would not have given the caseworker the right to treat me the way he did. I needed help, not judgment.)

Meanwhile, I had intended to stay at my aunt's house temporarily and planned to return to Southern Victoria High School, or SVHS, back in Canada. The first plan my aunt and I discussed was for me to live with my maternal grandparents. My mother then elected to tell me that her father had sexually abused her and raped her when she was nine.

Are you kidding me? My mother had let me stay at my grandparents' house for many weekends and parts of the summer. I was super close to my grandfather, and this shocked and horrified me. Not long afterward, when a family member confronted him about it, my grandfather looked ill when he found out what my mother had disclosed to me.

Although the issue eventually seemed to shrink away, it was never gone completely and our relationship was never the same again. In early adulthood, I cut him out of my life; I had told him if he wanted me in his life, he would need to go to counseling. He chose not to.

My next plan was to move in with one of my teachers at SVHS who had offered to take me in. Then during the winter break, she worked things out with her estranged spouse and called me to tell me the move was off. I was devastated. I felt rejection, confusion, and worry.

My aunt stepped in again. She told me they would switch rooms around, add a bed for me, and that I could stay. I'd be switching schools — and moving from Canada to the U.S. — but I felt relief, hope, and safety. I also didn't quite belong. I don't think anyone meant for me to feel that way; it is a sensitive area if you talk with anyone raised by relatives other than their parents.

As for my mother, I'm not sure what she did the afternoon I ran away but she did move back in with my father. Later, they knocked the wall down to take away my room and make my brother's room larger.

A New School And Life

I started Fort Fairfield High School after winter break of ninth grade and threw myself into my schoolwork. School has always been a safe and positive place for me. I loved learning, spending time with my peers, and became more involved with extracurricular activities. I made some poor choices (mostly with dating) but overall, I thrived in school.

I knew that I needed and wanted a better life. Despite my home life, I did have positive role models along the way; my parents had siblings who all appeared to live more normal lives with stable jobs, food, etc.

In addition to my Aunt Diane and Uncle Cookie, who took me in and loved me unconditionally, my Aunt Linda and Uncle Gene put Christmas gifts under our tree, and my Aunt Doris took excellent care of my paternal grandparents.

Aunt Sylvia and Uncle Dawson wrote amazing Christmas letters about all of their extensive travels and I knew that I wanted to do that too. Uncle Dale was an entrepreneur who was business savvy and worked hard. Three other uncles all held jobs and took care of their families.

Van, the woman from church, worked with me after I ran away. I was baptized, made my first communion, and was confirmed all in the same year — ninth grade.

So with those models, along with my own grit and commitment, I worked and studied throughout high school. I committed to go to college despite a lack of money.

One of my happiest moments was when my aunt called me at work my senior year to tell me that with grants and scholarships, I was attending University for free. Thank you, God, for getting me through. I was the first person in my family to go to college; later, I also went to grad school.

Where We Are Today

I graduated with my bachelor's and master's degrees in Social Work and have had a thriving career as a federal social worker serving active duty military, veterans, and their families. I've been a school therapist and a Christian Counselor. My therapy skills are powerful. I'm a lifelong learner who reads prolifically.

I've also assisted with multiple adoptions, including in my own family — I adopted my middle child — and I've traveled extensively. Just like I swore I would.

My biggest career success is truly helping others who have suffered from trauma. I compassionately hold parts of their stories to encourage their steps towards healing. With God's help, I'm able to be a safe connection and offer hope.

My biggest personal success is the family I created. It is multicultural, blended, and imperfect. My children experience love, safety, and security. They live with plenty of food, clothes, running water, and books. They love being home. Now, so do I!

Therapy has been instrumental in my journey. The social worker of my childhood did not stop me from getting help — I knew he was an anomaly. I attended therapy for the first time in college, intending to work on my baggage. However, I was close to graduating with my Master's and was prepping for a monumental move to Washington, D.C. Overwhelmed, my several sessions focused on this life transition.

My second time in therapy was marital counseling with my first spouse and lasted just two unhelpful sessions. Finally, my third therapy experience proved fruitful. I had an exceptional therapist — also named Karen — who I went to when my second marriage became rocky.

The tears I spilled in her office! She helped me let go of guilt for not wanting to spend time with my parents. She helped me when that second marriage was also falling apart. She told me about a book, "Parenting from the Inside Out," by Daniel Siegal that was so powerful for me. I completed every journaling exercise and learned more about how the brain changes by trauma. It was very healing for me as I learned how to re-parent myself.

As for my immediate family, my brother was a bit of a terror during adolescence with drugs, minor crimes, and some jail time. He told me that he felt abandoned when I ran away from home, which felt horrible to hear because I love him and did not want him to have pain. He has grown up to be a wonderful man and lives with his wife and children in Florida.

My mother finally left my father in 2017. My father threatened to kill her with his rifle, and she beat him to it and took a fistful of her meds. There is no psychiatric unit at the local hospital, and they sent her home to my dismay. My brother and I intervened with RCMP (Royal Canadian Mounted Police) and requested that the hospital hold her until I could get a flight to pick her up, but with no unit available, she was home before my plane arrived.

She was home packing, and I moved her to Virginia with me. I worked hard to get her everything she could need, including outstanding health care, senior services, and excellent therapy. With the help of her new doctor, we weaned her off of narcotics and benzos. Ultimately, she returned to her home. Just a few weeks later, she moved out into her own apartment. She realized that he was not willing to change, and that she deserved a better life. And she followed through with a divorce in July 2020; I'm so proud of her.

My father remains alone in his residence in Rowena. He remains in contact with my brother, but does not seem interested in me or his grandchildren. I'm at peace with his decision, as I can't see him changing at this late age unless he wants to. He does not.

It's unfortunate that he never wanted much out of life. He grew up with a learning disability, and it was difficult for him to get his GED. He also suffers from anxiety and chain smokes in an attempt to keep himself calm. I bought him everything he needed to quit smoking after he had a heart attack in 2009, but he didn't stick to it. I'm guessing he will smoke himself to death.

My aunt and uncle who helped raise me split their time between Florida and Maine. They did more for me than I could list here. They fed, clothed, and loved me. My uncle patiently taught me how to drive and was encouraging. My aunt, through her actions, showed me what it means to work hard and to be selfless. Her children were everything to her and she busted her butt for them (and me). I like to think I do the same for my children.

If I could dedicate this chapter to anyone, it would be to my Aunt Diane and Uncle Cookie (Hector) Cyr. They are genuine heroes.

Through everything, God would not give up on me, even when I strolled away. He always allowed me to come back into his open arms.

And finally, I've always had my dreams. I can create my own dreams with vision, thoughts, faith, and by taking action steps to be the best version of myself. I dream to be abundant in every area of my life, and this dream is coming true.

Karen Robinson is a licensed clinical social worker in Virginia with 22-plus years of experience. She works full time as a therapist and supervisory social worker with the Department of Defense. Karen recently started a new company with her daughters, called "Heal Thrive Dream, LLC," to serve trauma survivors and make a larger, global impact with women and children.

HealThriveDream.com

NEXT STEPS

No Bears Required

Therese Sparkins

I'm proud of you. In reaching the final chapter of this book, you've invested time in yourself. The question remains: What impact will these stories have in your life? What does all of this mean to you?

Kelly McCausey began this book by sharing how she got past her shit. She mentioned a retreat she attended called Radical Leadership, which I have had the privilege of leading since 2008. It's my wish that one day you and I will have a similar opportunity to engage at a deeper level like Kelly and countless others have.

For now, in the final pages of this book, I'll introduce you to the same tools and ideas that Kelly experienced. I have no doubt that this chapter, along with the examples shared in the previous pages, will put you on the path to get past your shit – fast.

First, take a moment to breathe and relish in the reflection of all that you have just read. There is a lot to unpack.

You just read stories about how nineteen inspirational people got past their shit.

This chapter is designed for you to take the lens through which you are looking at those stories and focus it back on your life. To create awareness around what reading these stories means for you.

In order to do that we will take a look at:

- why reading these stories sets the stage for you to create your dream life,

- the first simple shifts you can make to get past any of your own shit that is keeping you from what you want,
- and the invitation these authors are sending you.

I love exploring these three ideas for you because, as an executive coach, I'm constantly in awe of the rapid transformation that happens in the people who commit to this exploration.

There is something sacred about being able to witness the humanity and greatness of others the way you have had the opportunity to do while reading this book. Did you feel it?

It is a drawing back of the proverbial curtain that our Ego tells us we must hide behind to stay safe. You have witnessed others courageously stepping into the light to share their stories. Now you are invited to do the same. Let this chapter be a place where you take the time to look behind the curtain in your own life to see yourself authentically and love yourself unconditionally.

Each chapter displays the courage, tenacity, and resilience of a fellow human being. This is Essence in action. Remember how Kelly outlined Ego and Essence at the beginning of this book? Essence is awe-inspiring. Essence is breathtakingly simple. Essence is love. In each chapter, you had the gift of experiencing the Essence of another soul.

While Essence is inclusive and loving, Ego is fear and separateness. Both Essence and Ego have been present in the recounting of these stories. Each individual had their own unique brand of shit to get over.

A little background: notice I used the term unique, not "special." It is the Ego that wants to convince me my baggage is "special" and that I am the only one who is this terrible, broken, messed up, and unworthy. It sets up a comparison and makes me separate from others. The consequence of this erroneous way of thinking is that my shit becomes an overwhelming problem I need to struggle against on my own to solve. The result is that I feel isolated and remain stuck.

Therese Kienast, the founder of Radical Leadership, says, "You are not special, but you are precious."

While it is the Ego that wants you to be separate and special, your Essence understands that it does not have to go anywhere, do anything, or be anything different; you are already precious and deserving of unconditional love.

Think of the miraculousness of a newborn baby, already full of joy, promise, delight, and infinite possibilities. Your having lived on this planet for a few decades has not changed how precious you are. You've simply had more opportunities to forget this simple truth.

Because the Ego's job is to survive, it tries to convince you that the Ego itself is paramount to your survival. It does not want to be challenged, stretched, or let go of. Therefore, the Ego wants to convince you that you need to change. It wants to convince you that you have no choice but to work harder and be better, in order to be complete, happy and whole.

If the Ego can establish this as true, it can ensure its own survival because you will need it to fix yourself, analyze your faults, and dwell on the past. It sends you the message that you are broken and you must change to be worthy. Essence, on the other hand, KNOWS that you are already whole and precious. Just as you are.

Though you are naturally precious, perhaps you have created adaptations in order to survive that are no longer serving you. The good news is that when you are clear about what you want, and you find a gap between that vision and the current impact you are having, you do not have to change. You can simply make new choices that align with the impact you do want. No fixing, hard work, or judgment needed.

All of these stories contained unique circumstances and yet each individual was having an entirely *human* experience.

The range of experiences varied, from Nicole Dean's battle with anxiety and depression to Lane Therrell's abusive relationship; or from Michelle Garrett's suicide attempt to Tishia Lee's alcoholism, and Benecia Ponder's loss of eyesight.

While the content in each experience was vastly different, the Essence of the stories had a clear theme: the indomitable human spirit. Each of these women faced and overcame her circumstances by putting Essence in the driver's seat and returning to her natural state of being. And even though the circumstances were challenging, complex, and a huge invitation to live in fear (where Ego runs the show), these women chose something different. They leaned in on their inner-knowing. They leaned in on their Spirit, their Essence.

Taking The First Step

At their core, each of these women had everything they ever needed to make it through the shit life threw their way and come out creating what they wanted. It may be hard to believe in this moment, but I'm happy to report that you too already have everything you will ever need to get over any of the baggage you may still be carrying with you.

Perhaps you felt sadness or the fear of familiarity wash over you as you read through these pages. Or maybe you felt excited as you recognized places in your life where you have already let go of some of your own shit. You may have even had moments where you did not fully understand someone's experience.

No matter what your experience has been while reading, it is perfect! You are right where you are meant to be in this moment.

Wherever you are, and whatever experience you had while reading this book, use it now to create awareness.

Creating awareness is THE most powerful thing you can do to get over, get past, or even choose to love your shit.

Awareness is the act of slowing down and holding up the magnifying glass to your life. Like a private eye investigates and objectively observes what is taking place, Awareness simply gets curious and takes notes. You examine things in new ways and "see" the Truth of things you have not "seen" before.

Awareness is key.

As Kelly mentioned in the opening chapter, the Ego is designed to keep us safe. It is a mechanism that was put in place for our survival. So Ego can be useful.

Unfortunately, the Ego is like the artificial intelligence in a dystopian sci-fi flick that gets a mind of its own and takes over. As we have evolved, the Ego has gone into overdrive and often shows up to protect us when we don't need protecting.

Without reflection, without slowing down to create awareness, Ego has us "seeing" a distorted version of reality. It has us responding to threats that may not actually be threatening.

Did you know that physiologically it does not matter whether you are in the presence of a hungry bear that is going to eat you or whether you simply *think and believe* that you see a bear? Your body will respond in exactly the same way!

The Ego (bless its heart) was designed to be something that supports our survival. It was designed to pop in every once in a while to send up a flare, warning us of actual existential threats. However, while our modern world has become a relatively safe place, the Ego still wants to prove itself useful. Now, instead of simply flagging life-threatening warnings, it flags a whole host of things that it wants us to perceive as dangerous.

It does not matter whether the threat is a sideways glance from a colleague, a snotty remark from a teenager, the idea to let go of a part of a business or something that once worked, OR a real live grizzly bear ready to attack. Any one of these scenarios can feel threatening without awareness.

No matter how big or small the threat, Ego goes into survival mode and creates feelings of pain and terror to provoke us into seeking safety.

Without awareness, the experience of my reaction and the reality I hold as true make it feel real for me.

No matter what shit you are carrying around, your body and brain believe *you see a bear.*

Fortunately, there is hope. Awareness shines a light on what the Ego is trying to keep me safe from. It creates the space to question the severity of the threat and decide what (if anything) to do about it. This offers freedom from the tyranny of hijacked thoughts.

For awareness to do its job at keeping Ego in check, it requires an essential ingredient: grace.

Grace is a component that I used to skip over (and still sometimes do), but it's crucial to creating awareness and sustainably getting over my shit.

Without grace, judgment stops awareness in its tracks. It is important to note that while others can sometimes be an invitation for me to question myself, the most damaging judgments usually come from within. I become aware of how I am creating an impact that I do not want, I take something personally, and instead of being able to make a shift and do something about it, I head straight into a downward spiral of self flagellation and condemnation.

There's that bear again.

Why would I continue to be curious and create awareness if it always feels so painful? So in my avoidance of pain, I stick my head in the sand and the Ego does its best to keep me "safe."

Awareness In Action

Have you ever had an experience where you "woke up" to a negative impact you were having and immediately wanted to crawl in a hole or start looking for excuses to make yourself feel better?

One such experience in my life came while I was sitting in a quaint stonewalled pub in Germany. I was having a conversation with a good friend about some challenging things and a potential divorce unfolding in his life. We were about an hour and a half into our conversation when the server brought a piece of paper over to our table and dropped it off. She noted that the couple just walking out wanted her to deliver it. The note read: "Thank you for talking so loud that we were in every part of your conversation. You ruined our meal."

As I read the note, the blood drained from my face and I instantly identified this as one of the most embarrassing experiences of my life.

The world seemed to stand still while my thoughts raced. I wanted to crumple up the paper and not mention it to my friend for fear that he would jump on the bandwagon and get upset with my volume level or mad that I had been "airing his dirty laundry."

At that moment my Ego *thought it saw a bear.*

Ego told me that I was in danger of losing a friend, that everyone in the restaurant hated me, and as a result I would no doubt be reduced to living in a van down by the river. The Ego has a funny way of doing that: creating an entire story that leaves my life in ruins over one small incident.

In the grips of that moment I created so many thoughts to make my bruised and afraid Ego feel better. First, I wrote it off to cultural differences, then I blamed it on the echos off the stone walls. Next, I got angry that they sent such a passive aggressive note when they could have asked me to turn down my volume so much sooner and avoided this embarrassment altogether. Finally, I wanted to ignore the note and dismiss it as being written by someone crazy.

All of these thoughts ran through my mind in mere seconds (Ego can be very efficient!).

Fortunately, I didn't hold on to any of those thoughts for long. I let them go.

By the grace of God and the practice of creating awareness, this moment was different than other moments of panic and embarrassment in my life.

This time, I took a deep breath and got curious like a detective. I asked myself, did I want to have the impact of being disruptive and so loud that other people around me had no choice but to be included in my conversations? The answer was no. (In contrast, remember when Val Selby investigated the impact that she was having when she received the feedback of being too loud? When she held up her magnifying glass, she discovered that her volume was usually working for her.)

Then I asked myself, is it possible that the feedback was legit, even if it was delivered in a way that sent me on tilt?

As I considered this question, I noted that there were a few other times in the past when I had received feedback on my overzealous volume, so this was not an isolated incident. This is important to investigate because as Val mentioned in her story, people project things they don't like about themselves onto others all the time. So with my detective work, I wanted to determine whether this particular feedback was about me, about them, or about both of us.

One of the greatest ways I have been able to determine which of these possibilities is the culprit comes from a bit of wisdom based on an ancient Chinese proverb. *If **one** person calls you a horse's ass, ignore them. If **two** people call you a horse's ass, take a look in the mirror. If **three** people call you a horse's ass, go buy a saddle.* Given the multiple times I had received the feedback, it was time for me to buy a saddle. I was not creating the impact I wanted.

NOTE OF CAUTION: Remember, you are the navigator of your own ship. You are the detective holding up the magnifying glass. You are ultimately the one who decides if your impact is what you want or not. Do not just accept feedback from three people without first pausing to create awareness.

As I slowed down and started to look, I was creating awareness. I was holding up that magnifying glass. But the component that allowed me to look and not be paralyzed in fear, to not hide in shame, was Grace.

The racing thoughts stopped and I took a deep breath. I felt the blood return to my face and I had a sense of peace and calm. There was no bear.

This was simply new information and feedback for me to consider how I wanted to continue moving forward. A way for me to recalibrate and come closer to creating more of the impact that I want to be having in the world.

Grace becomes possible when I trust that I am doing the best I can with what I have at any given moment. Similar to Val, I came by being loud honestly. Just like the food that goes into our bodies provides us nutrients, at one point in my past, the behavior of being loud served me. I come from a family of extroverted, loud and fast talkers (my parents themselves grew up with seven and nine siblings each). Chaos ensues at every family meal and social gathering.

In order to be heard, I had cultivated a way of speaking up so others would tune in and listen. At one point in my past, speaking loudly had the impact I wanted. It got me the attention I was craving.

Then, just like the food that we put into our bodies for nutrition ultimately becomes waste (AKA our shit), so do the past behaviors and patterns that once served us. Now, in this moment, as a guest in this foreign country, it was clear that the volume of my voice was no longer having the impact that I wanted.

There was no judgment or condemnation for myself in that awareness; these were simply the facts. Things that I had never slowed down to pay attention to and evaluate before. But with this awareness, I was able to face my fear, turn to my friend, and share what the note said.

As you have been reading, perhaps your Ego is whispering, "Sure, awareness worked in this example, Therese, but this is a 'small potatoes' example."

I want to caution you against comparing the weightiness of shit. Other people's, and yours.

Throughout this book, you've read about some pretty big shit people have overcome. But this combative dance between Ego, awareness, and grace can appear within the mundane, too. That's what makes it such a fascinating discovery. And when you see how easily you can handle it in relatively smaller situations, it becomes easier to turn to awareness and grace in any situation.

I chose this example not because the content is earth-shattering, but because of the context. Cultivating the ability to slow things down, hold up the magnifying glass, create awareness, and not take things personally (big or small) has transformed my life.

Please note: I did not have to work hard to "change" myself. Rather, in a flash, I was able to create awareness with grace that revealed the clarity for what was naturally next for me.

Awareness with grace in this minor situation brought me freedom in all situations.

One of my favorite quotes to share in Radical Leadership comes from Gloria Steinem: "The Truth will set you free; but it will piss you off first."

In those first few moments after receiving the feedback, I felt pissed! But then I felt free. Free to let go of this specific adaptation that I had been holding onto for so long. Free to be more me. Free to let go of my shit.

Imagine the power Awareness can have in your life if I can feel this much freedom over letting go of the "small potatoes shit" of being too loud. I want that for you. Freedom and the ability to clearly know what is natural and next for you.

Ego's Trick: Dirty Little Secrets

Another game that the Ego plays is, "If I don't look at it, talk about it, or acknowledge it, the problem doesn't exist."

The Ego operates as if this is true (wouldn't it be nice if it was?). Rather than being effective, this technique often tucks things in the back of the mind as dirty little secrets, while the impact and judgment carried around about these secrets mounts.

These become the things that the Ego blackmails us into silence with: "You had better not let anyone know that or they will never accept you or love you."

This Ego tactic was in full force when I received a letter from a client I was about to bring on board. The letter was a ten-page confessional about all of the "baggage" she was carrying around. The shame she dared not speak out loud or share with another soul in fear that she would be dismissed, judged, and sent the message (yet again) that she was broken beyond repair.

As I read on, with each new "secret" she exposed I felt even closer to her. I got to hear what was real in her life and witness all of the bears that her Ego was seeing. I noticed how scary and alone it must have felt to try to keep all of this hidden and tucked away. When I read the last few lines of her letter my heart sank to the floor. She said, "I am pretty sure I am beyond help so if you can not help me and do not want to be my coach, I completely understand."

She was so paralyzed by these thoughts and judgments of herself that she was convinced if anyone else were to hear them all, they too would judge her the way she condemned and judged herself. I felt a peace fall over me and an overwhelming compassion for just how scared and alone this woman felt. What I felt was God's love; it was unconditional love.

Have you ever had the thought, *"What if somebody knew... would they still love me?"*

Have you ever felt the pressure to keep people from finding something out about you and had to make concessions to manage your image?

From the bottom of my heart and from my soul to yours: You are loved. As a matter of fact, Love, Joy, Surprise, and Delight are your NATURAL state of being. If you ever feel anything other than that, your Ego and patterns are running the show.

There is nothing in this world that you could do or say to be unlovable. You were born worthy, you are enough, and you are loved.

An Invitation To Try Something Different

Let your reading of this book be a turning point where you bring the thoughts, things, and autopilot patterns that you are running into the light. Get curious about this stuff that you have been carrying around and investigate whether it still serves you.

If it is no longer working for you, my invitation is to try something different. Anything different. Then check in to see if *that* creates more of what you want.

Ultimately, each soul represented in these stories was able to let go of their shit to create what they want in the world. This is exponentially good news!

Not only have these people been able to cultivate more joy and happiness in their own lives, but their contentment and joy are contagious. Their clarity is exponential!

By taking the time to create Awareness, unveil the Ego, and have the courage to share their experience publicly, these women are sending you an invitation to join in. An invitation to let go of anything holding you back, to let go of your shit and live your life from love, joy, surprise, and delight.

Can you imagine the void in this world if Kelly McCausey had wallowed in self-judgment and never cultivated the grace to unconditionally love herself? She might never have developed Love People and Make Money, and you might not be reading this book right now.

Reading these stories and reflecting on humanity calls you forth to create Awareness and be the most powerful you that you can be, living from your Essence. Your Essence is the foundation for you to create the life of your dreams. And by doing so, *you* invite others to do the same.

Truly, exponential impact.

Kelly's success and celebration create exponential impact, they beckon your Essence, your inner knowing that there is more, and they invite you to take the next step. The next step for you is to let go of your shit and choose to live from your unconditionally loving Essence.

Have you ever read a book that you just KNEW had the potential to change your life, and you did nothing? The book may have contained some of the most mind-blowing principles and they resonated for you, and yet life went right back to normal just as soon as you closed the back cover. Unfortunately, this is all too common an experience.

Remember what Kelly said in the beginning: Ego is running the show 98 percent of the time! This means that we are running in survival mode, checking off our to-do lists, hamster-wheeling on autopilot virtually all of the time.

We are fish swimming in the water of Ego. From time to time we jump up and get a flash out of water, we get a glimpse of our natural Essence and the power of who we are designed to be. Then right back into the water we go.

So What, Now What?

"So what, now what?" is another phrase I love to use within Radical Leadership that captures why Awareness is so powerful. By stopping to investigate what is True (with a capital T), I can now look forward and choose what action steps to take next.

There is an action you can take right now to increase the odds that things will not default back to "life as usual."

You can decide to do something different, anything different. Then, after a short while, spend time reflecting on whether that creates more of the impact that you want. Whatever you do, take action.

If you feel at a loss for where to start and know that you would like more direction, Kelly has promised a workbook as a self-coaching resource to help you begin the process of creating awareness around the shit that may have been running you. Have the courage now to download and go through it. Take the one small step that will transform your world forever.

Finally, always remember as you play with uncovering the shit you carry (the heavy, the insignificant, and everything in between) that the key component of awareness is Grace. It is this unconditional love that sets you free to get over your shit.

No actual bears required.

An Executive coach and Radical Leadership workshop facilitator, Therese Sparkins is a stand for your life to be filled with love, joy, surprise, and delight on a daily basis.

ThereseSparkins.com

Claim Your Free Self-Coaching Workbook
At GetPastYourShit.com